A SHORTER
PRAYER DURING THE DAY

Other editions of *The Divine Office* available

The Divine Office, complete in 3 volumes
Daily Prayer
Morning and Evening Prayer
Evening Prayer for Sundays
Night Prayer (Compline)
Readings for Lent
Parish Sunday Vespers (musical settings)
A Shorter Morning and Evening Prayer
A Shorter Morning and Evening Prayer (large print edition)

A SHORTER
PRAYER DURING THE DAY

The Psalter of
The Divine Office

with selected texts for the Seasons,
Feasts of the Lord, and Solemnities

COLLINS

Taken from *The Divine Office*, a translation of *Liturgia Horarum*, approved by the Episcopal Conferences of Australia, England and Wales, Ireland, Scotland.

Also approved for use in Gambia, Ghana, India, Kenya, Liberia, Malaysia and Singapore, New Zealand, Nigeria, Sierra Leone, Tanzania, Uganda and Zimbabwe.

Concordat cum originali: John P Dewis
Denis J Hart

Nihil obstat: Anton Cowan
Imprimatur: Ralph Brown, VG
Westminster, 26 November, 1985

ISBN 0 00 599910 3
Printed in Great Britain by
William Collins Sons & Co Ltd,
Glasgow

CONTENTS

ACKNOWLEDGEMENTS

The Publishers are grateful to the following for permission to reproduce copyright material.

SCRIPTURE TEXTS

The following versions have been used:
Knox Bible, © 1945, 1949, the Hierarchy of England and Wales.
New English Bible, 2nd edition copyright 1970, Oxford and Cambridge University Presses.
Revised Standard Version, Common Bible, copyrighted © 1973, by the Division of Christian Education, National Council of the Churches of Christ in the USA. Special permission has been obtained to use in this publication the 'you-your-yours' forms of the personal pronoun in the address of God.
Today's English Version (Good News for Modern Man), United Bible Societies of America and Collins Publishers, London.
Psalm texts are translated from the Hebrew by The Grail, © The Grail (England) 1963, and published by Collins. They are reprinted from the Singing Version first published in Fontana Books in 1966.
The practical needs of choral recitation prompted a number of revisions in the psalms and canticles of this Breviary. These revisions are made with the agreement of The Grail.

HYMNS

The hymns are reproduced from *Stanbrook Abbey Hymnal* by permission of the Benedictine Nuns of Stanbrook Abbey.

PREFACE

This book contains a selection of material from Prayer During the Day from *The Divine Office.* It may serve as a convenient pocket companion for travellers who would normally use either *Daily Prayer* or *The Divine Office* in its complete form. It may also be used when groups of Christians – lay and clerical, and perhaps from various denominations – meet during the day: for example as prayer before meetings, or for a period of recollection and meditation based on psalmody and the hearing of the word of God.

It contains:

- the complete Four Week Psalter for Prayer during the Day
- sufficient material from the Proper of Seasons to allow for seasonal variation: a week of proper material for each of the Seasons; and for Christmas Day,* Palm Sunday,*, Good Friday and Easter Sunday*
- for the Feasts of the Lord and Solemnities during the Seasonal Cycle or in Ordinary Time, and for Solemnities from the General Calendar of Saints, the whole Prayer is given
- the Office for the Dead

*which may be used during the octave.

STRUCTURE OF PRAYER DURING THE DAY

INTRODUCTION

℣ O God, come to our aid.
℟ O Lord, make haste to help us.
Glory be to the Father and to the Son and to the Holy Spirit, as it was in the beginning, is now, and ever shall be, world without end. Amen. Alleluia.

HYMN

PSALMODY

Antiphon
Psalm
Antiphon

SCRIPTURE READING

Versicle and Response

CONCLUDING PRAYER

CONCLUSION

Let us praise the Lord.
℟ Thanks be to God.

THE CYCLE OF THE FOUR WEEK PSALTER

Each year, begin using Psalter Week 1 on:

First Sunday of Advent
Monday after the Baptism of the Lord
First Sunday of Lent
Easter Sunday

Each year on Monday after Pentecost, examine this TABLE and begin using Psalter of the appropriate week as follows:

YEAR	PSALTER WEEK	YEAR	PSALTER WEEK
1986	3	1993	1
1987	2	1994	4
1988	4	1995	1
1989	2	1996	4
1990	1	1997	3
1991	3	1998	1
1992	2	1999	4

THE PSALTER

WEEK 1: SUNDAY

℣ O God, come to our aid.
℟ O Lord, make haste to help us.
Glory be to the Father and to the Son and to the Holy Spirit, as it was in the beginning, is now, and ever shall be, world without end. Amen. Alleluia.

HYMN

O blessèd Lord, Creator God,
In you all things are rendered pure,
By you are strengthened to endure.

O blessèd, holy hand of God,
All things are sanctified by you;
Adorned, enriched, you make them new.

O blessèd Majesty of God,
Containing all that you have filled;
All things are done as you have willed.

O blessèd, holy Trinity,
Serene and certain in your ways;
You are the light of endless days.

The hymn given for Sunday may be used on each day of the week following. If desired, other suitable hymns may be used.
If three Hours of this Prayer are said: at one Hour, the psalms are said as below; at the other Hours, the complementary psalms are used: see pp. 123 ff.

PSALMODY

The antiphons for Advent, Christmastide and Lent are given in the Proper of Seasons.
Ant. Eastertide: Alleluia, alleluia, alleluia.
Ant. 1: It is good to find refuge in the Lord; his love endures for ever, alleluia.

SONG OF REJOICING IN SALVATION PSALM 117(118)
This is the stone which was rejected by you builders, but which has become the corner stone (Acts 4:11)

I

Give thánks to the Lórd for he is good,*
for his lóve endures for éver.

Let the sóns of Ísrael sáy:*
'His lóve endures for éver.'
Let the sóns of Áaron say:*
'His lóve endures for éver.'
Let thóse who fear the Lórd sáy:*
'His lóve endures for éver.'

I cálled to the Lórd in my distréss;*
he ánswered and fréed me.
The Lórd is at my síde; I do not féar.*
What can mán do agáinst me?
The Lórd is at my síde as my hélper:*
I shall look dówn on my fóes.

It is bétter to take réfuge in the Lórd*
than to trúst in mén:
it is bétter to take réfuge in the Lórd*
than to trúst in prínces.

Glory be to the Father and to the Son and to the Holy Spirit,*
As it was in the beginning, is now, and ever shall be, world without end. Amen.

This doxology is said after each psalm and canticle unless otherwise noted.

Ant. It is good to find refuge in the Lord; his love endures for ever, alleluia.
Ant. 2: The Lord is my strength and my song, alleluia.

II

The nátions áll encómpassed me;*
in the Lórd's name I crúshed them.
They cómpassed me, cómpassed me abóut;*
in the Lórd's name I crúshed them.
They cómpassed me abóut like bées;†
they blázed like a fíre among thórns.*
In the Lórd's name I crúshed them.

I was hárd-préssed and was fálling*
but the Lórd came to hélp me.
The Lórd is my stréngth and my sóng;*
hé is my sáviour.
There are shóuts of jóy and víctory*
in the ténts of the júst.

The Lórd's right hánd has tríumphed;*
his ríght hand ráised me.
The Lórd's right hánd has tríumphed;†
I shall not díe, I shall líve*
and recóunt his déeds.
I was púnished, I was púníshed by the Lórd,*
but nót doomed to díe.

Ant. The Lord is my strength and my song, alleluia.
Ant. 3: I will praise you, Lord, for you have answered me, alleluia.

III

Ópen to mé the gates of hóliness:*
I will énter and give thánks.
Thís is the Lórd's own gáte*
where the júst may énter.
I will thánk you for yóu have ánswered*
and yóu are my sáviour.

The stóne which the buílders rejécted*
has becóme the córner stone.
Thís is the wórk of the Lórd,*
a márvel in our éyes.
Thís day was máde by the Lórd;*
we rejóice and are glád.

O Lórd, gránt us salvátion;*
O Lórd, grant succéss.
Bléssed in the náme of the Lórd*
is hé who cómes.
We bléss you from the hóuse of the Lórd;*
the Lord Gód is our líght.

Go fórward in procéssion with bránches*
éven to the áltar.
Yóu are my Gód, I thánk you.*
My Gód, I práise you.
Give thánks to the Lórd for he is góod;*
for his lóve endures for éver.

Ant. I will praise you, Lord, for you have answered me, alleluia.
Eastertide: Alleluia, alleluia, alleluia.

Through the Year

Before Noon

SCRIPTURE READING 1 JN 4:16

We ourselves have known and put our faith in God's love towards ourselves. God is love and anyone who lives in love lives in God, and God lives in him.

℣ Bend my heart to your will, O God.
℟ By your word, give me life.

Midday

SCRIPTURE READING GAL 6:8

A man will reap what he sows; if nature is his seed-ground, nature will give him a perishable harvest, if his seed-ground is the spirit, it will give him a harvest of eternal life.

℣ Your word, O Lord, stands firm for ever.
℟ Your truth lasts from age to age.

Afternoon

SCRIPTURE READING GAL 6:9-10

Let us not be discouraged over our acts of charity; we shall reap when the time comes, if we persevere in them. Let us practise generosity to all, while the opportunity is ours; and above all, to those who are of one family with us in the faith.

℣ I called with all my heart; Lord, hear me.
℟ I will keep your commandments.

The concluding prayer from the Proper of Seasons.

Conclusion

When no other Hour follows and at least in communal recitation:

Let us praise the Lord.
℟ Thanks be to God.

WEEK 1: MONDAY

Hymn *(see p. 9)*

PSALMODY

In Advent, Christmastide and Lent the antiphons are proper.

Ant. Eastertide: Alleluia, alleluia, alleluia.
Ant. 1: The Lord's precepts are right and good: joy for the heart, light for the eyes.

PRAISE TO GOD, THE LORD OF THE LAW PSALM 18(19)B:8-15

Be perfect as your Father in heaven is perfect (Mt 5:48)

The láw of the Lórd is pérfect,*
it revíves the sóul.
The rúle of the Lórd is to be trústed,*
it gives wísdom to the símple.

The précepts of the Lórd are ríght,*
they gládden the héart.
The commánd of the Lórd is cléar,*
it gives líght to the éyes.

The féar of the Lórd is hóly,*
abíding for éver.
The decrées of the Lórd are trúth*
and áll of them júst.

They are móre to be desíred than góld,
than the púrest of góld
and swéeter are théy than hóney,*
than hóney from the cómb.

So in thém your sérvant finds instrúction;*
great rewárd is in their kéeping.
But whó can detéct all his érrors?*
From hídden faults acquít me.

From presúmption restráin your sérvant*
and lét it not rúle me.
Thén shall Í be bláme!ess,*
cléan from grave sín.

May the spóken wórds of my móuth,*
the thóughts of my héart,
win fávour in your síght, O Lórd,*
my réscuer, my róck!

Ant. The Lord's precepts are right and good: joy for the heart, light for the eyes.
Ant. 2: The Lord will arise as righteous judge of the peoples.

THE PRAYER OF THE INNOCENT MAN SUBJECTED TO SLANDER — PSALM 7

Behold, the judge is standing at the door (Jas 5:9)

I

Lord Gód, I take réfuge in yóu.*
From my pursúer sáve me and réscue me,

lest he téar me to píeces like a líon*
and drag me óff with nó one to réscue me.

Lord Gód, if my hánds have done wróng,†
if I have páid back évil for góod,*
I who sáved my unjúst oppréssor:
then let my fóe pursúe me and séize me,†
let him trámple my lífe to the gróund*
and láy my sóul in the dúst.

Lórd, rise úp in your ánger,†
ríse against the fúry of my fóes;*
my God, awáke! Yóu will give júdgment.

Let the cómpany of nátions gather róund you,†
taking your séat abóve them on hígh.*
The Lórd is júdge of the péoples.

Give júdgment for me, Lórd; I am júst†
and ínnocent of héart.*
Put an énd to the évil of the wícked!
Make the júst stand fírm,†
you who tést mínd and héart,*
O júst Gód!

Ant. The Lord will arise as righteous judge of the peoples.
Ant. 3: How just a judge God is, how strong: he saves the upright of heart.

II

Gód is the shíeld that protécts me,*
who saves the úpright of héart.
Gód is a júst júdge*
slów to ánger;
but he thréatens the wícked every dáy,*
men who wíll not repént.

Gód will shárpen his swórd;*
he has bráced his bów and taken áim.
For thém he has prepáred deadly wéapons;*
he bárbs his árrows with fíre.

Here is óne who is prégnant with málice,*
conceives évil and bríngs forth líes.

He digs a pítfall, dígs it déep;*
and in the tráp he has máde he will fáll.
His málice will recóil on himsélf;*
on his ówn head his víolence will fáll.

I will thánk the Lórd for his jústice:*
I will síng to the Lórd, the Most Hígh.

Ant. How just a judge God is, how strong: he saves the upright of heart.
Eastertide: Alleluia, alleluia, alleluia.

At the other Hours, the complementary psalms.

Through the Year

Before Noon

SCRIPTURE READING ROM 13:8,10

Owe no one anything, except to love one another; for he who loves his neighbour has fulfilled the law. Love does no wrong to a neighbour; therefore love is the fulfilling of the law.

℣ You have been my help; do not abandon me.
℟ Do not forsake me, O God my help.

CONCLUDING PRAYER

Father, Creator of all that is good,
you have called men to work in your world,
and by their co-operation to better the condition of mankind.
Grant that we may always work together as children of your family,
and love all men as our brethren.
Through Christ our Lord.

Midday

SCRIPTURE READING JAS 1:19-20,26

It is for us men to be ready listeners, slow to speak our minds, slow to take offence; man's anger does not bear the fruit that is acceptable to God. If anyone deludes himself by thinking he is serving God, when he has not learned to control his tongue, the service he gives is vain.

℣ I will bless the Lord at all times.
℟ His praise will be always on my lips.

CONCLUDING PRAYER
God, Lord and master of the vineyard,
you allot us our tasks
and determine the just rewards of our labours.
Help us to bear the burden of the day
and accept your will in all things without complaint.
Through Christ our Lord.

Afternoon

SCRIPTURE READING 1 PET 1:17-18a, 19

Look anxiously to the ordering of your lives while your stay on earth lasts. What was the ransom that freed you? You know well enough that it was not paid in earthly currency, silver or gold; it was paid in the precious blood of Christ; no lamb was ever so pure, so spotless a victim.
℣ Redeem me, Lord, and show me your mercy.
℟ I will bless the Lord in the assembly.

CONCLUDING PRAYER
God our Father,
you are calling us to prayer,
at that same hour
when the apostles went up to the temple.
Grant that the prayer we offer with sincere hearts
in the name of Jesus,
may bring salvation to all who call upon that holy Name.
Through Christ our Lord.

WEEK 1: TUESDAY

Hymn *(see p. 9)*

PSALMODY

In Advent, Christmastide and Lent the antiphons are proper.

Ant. Eastertide: Alleluia, alleluia, alleluia.
Ant. 1: Blessed are they who live by the law of the Lord.

MEDITATION ON THE WORD OF GOD IN THE LAW — PSALM 118(119):1-8 I (ALEPH)

This is the love of God, that we keep his commandments (1 Jn 5:3)

They are háppy whose lífe is blámeless,*
who fóllow God's láw!
They are háppy who dó his wíll,*
seeking hím with all their héarts,
who néver do ánything évil*
but wálk in his wáys.

Yóu have laid dówn your précepts*
to be obéyed with cáre.
Máy my fóotsteps be fírm*
to obéy your rúlings.
Thén I shall nót be put to sháme*
as I héed your commánds.

I will thánk you with an úpright héart*
as I léarn your decrées.
Í will obéy your státutes:*
dó not forsáke me.

Ant. Blessed are they who live by the law of the Lord.
Ant. 2: My heart shall rejoice in your salvation.

LAMENTATION OF A JUST MAN WHO TRUSTS IN THE LORD

PSALM 12(13)

May the God of hope fill you with every joy (Rom 15:13)

How lóng, O Lórd, will yóu forgét me?*
How lóng wíll you híde your fáce?
How lóng must Í bear gríef in my sóul,†
this sórrow in my héart dáy and níght?*
How lóng sháll my énemy preváil?

Lóok at me, ánswer me, Lórd my Gód!*
Give líght to my éyes lest I fáll asleep in déath,
lest my énemy sáy: 'Í have overcóme him';*
lest my fóes rejóice to sée my fáll.

As for mé, I trúst in your mérciful lóve.*
Let my héart rejoíce in your sáving hélp:
Let me síng to the Lórd for his góodness to mé,*
singing psálms to the náme of the Lórd, the Most Hígh.

Ant. My heart shall rejoice in your salvation.
Ant 3: God made all men prisoners of disobedience, that he might show mercy to them all.

THE FOOLISHNESS OF SINNERS

PSALM 13(14)

Where sin increased, grace abounded all the more (Rom 5:20)

The fóol has sáid in his héart:*
'There is no Gód abóve.'
Their déeds are corrúpt, depráved;*
not a góod man is léft.

From héaven the Lórd looks dówn*
on the sóns of mén
to sée if ány are wíse,*
if ány seek Gód.

Áll have léft the right páth,*
depráved, every óne:

there is nót a góod man léft,*
nó, not even óne.

Will the évil-doers nót understánd?†
They éat up my péople
as thoúgh they were éating bréad:*
they never práy to the Lórd.

Sée how they trémble with féar†
without cáuse for féar:*
for Gód is with the júst.
You may móck the póor man's hópe,*
but his réfuge is the Lórd.

O that Ísrael's salvátion might cóme from Síon!†
When the Lórd delívers his péople from bóndage,*
then Jácob will be glád and Ísrael rejóice.

Ant. God made all men prisoners of disobedience, that he might show mercy to them all.
Eastertide: Alleluia, alleluia, alleluia.

At the other Hours, the complementary psalms.

Through the Year

Before Noon

SCRIPTURE READING JER 17:7-8

Blessed shall he be that puts his trust in the Lord, makes the Lord his refuge. Not more favoured is a tree planted by the water's edge, that pushes out its roots to catch the moisture, and defies the summer heat; its green leaves careless of the drought, its fruit unfailing.
℣ The Lord will not refuse any good to those who walk without blame.
℟ Lord, God of hosts, happy the man who trusts in you.

CONCLUDING PRAYER

Almighty ever-living God,
who at this hour sent down your Holy Spirit on the apostles,
send forth that same Spirit of love into our hearts
so that we may bear faithful witness to you,
before all mankind.
Through Christ our Lord.

Midday

SCRIPTURE READING PROV 3:13-15

Happy the man who discovers wisdom,
the man who gains discernment:
gaining her is more rewarding than silver,
more profitable than gold.
She is beyond the price of pearls,
nothing you could covet is her equal.
℣ Lord, you love truth in the heart.
℟ In my heart you have taught me wisdom.

CONCLUDING PRAYER

Almighty God,
who revealed to Peter your plan for the salvation of all men,
grant that our work may be acceptable to you,
and that, by your grace, it may further your loving purpose of redemption.
Through Christ our Lord.

Afternoon

SCRIPTURE READING JOB 5:17-18

Happy indeed the man whom God corrects!
Then do not refuse this lesson from the Lord.
For he who wounds is he who soothes the sore,
and the hand that hurts is the hand that heals.
℣ Treat your servant with love, Lord.
℟ Teach me your commandments.

CONCLUDING PRAYER

Almighty God,
we recall how you sent your angel to the centurion Cornelius
to show him the way of salvation.
Open our hearts to work more zealously
for the salvation of the world,
so that your Church
may bring us and all men into your presence.
Through Christ our Lord.

WEEK 1: WEDNESDAY

Hymn *(see p. 9)*

PSALMODY

In Advent, Christmastide and Lent the antiphons are proper.

Ant. Eastertide: Alleluia, alleluia, alleluia.
Ant. 1: Blessed are you, O Lord; teach me your commands.

PSALM 118(119):9-16 II (BETH)

Hów shall the yóung remain sínless?*
By obéying your wórd.
I have sóught you with áll my héart:*
let me not stráy from your commánds.

I tréasure your prómise in my héart*
lest I sín agáinst you.
Bléssed are yóu, O Lórd;*
téach me your commánds.

With my tóngue I have recóunted*
the decrées of your líps.
I rejóiced to dó your wíll*
as though all ríches were míne.

I will pónder áll your précepts*
and consíder your páths.
I táke delíght in your commánds;*
I will nót forget your wórd.

Ant. Blessed are you, O Lord; teach me your commands.
Ant. 2: Maintain my steps firm in your ways, Lord.

LORD, SAVE ME FROM EVIL MEN PSALM 16(17)

During his life on earth he offered up prayer, which was heard (Heb 5:7)

I

Lórd, hear a cáuse that is júst,*

pay héed to my crý.
Túrn your éar to my práyer:*
no decéit is on my líps.

From yóu may my júdgment come fórth.*
Your éyes discern the trúth.

You séarch my héart, you vísit me by níght.†
You tést me and you fínd in mé no wróng.*
My wórds are not sínful as are mén's wórds.

I képt from víolence becáuse of your wórd,†
I képt my féet fírmly in your páths;*
there wás no fáltering ín my stéps.

I am hére and I cáll, you will héar me, O Gód,*
Túrn your éar to me; héar my wórds.
Displáy your great lóve, yóu whose ríght hand sáves*
your friénds from thóse who rebél agáinst them.

Guárd me as the ápple of your éye.†
Híde me in the shádow of your wíngs*
from the víolent attáck of the wícked.

Ant. Maintain my steps firm in your ways, Lord.
Ant. 3: Lord, arise, rescue my soul.

II

My fóes encírcle me with déadly intént.†
Their héarts tight shút, their móuths speak próudly.*
They advánce agáinst me, and nów they surróund me.

Their éyes are wátching to stríke me to the gróund†
as thóugh they were líons réady to cláw*
or líke some young líon cróuched in híding.

Lord, aríse, confrónt them, stríke them dówn!*
Let your swórd réscue my soúl from the wícked;
let your hánd, O Lórd, réscue me from mén,*
from mén whose rewárd is in this présent life.

You gíve them their fíll of your tréasures;†

they rejóice in abúndance of óffspring*
and léave their wéalth to their chíldren.

As for mé, in my jústice I shall sée your fáce*
and be fílled, when I awáke, with the síght of your glóry.

Ant. Lord, arise, rescue my soul.
Eastertide: Alleluia, alleluia, alleluia.

At the other Hours, the complementary psalms.

Through the Year

Before Noon

SCRIPTURE READING 1 PET 1:13-14

Have your minds ready for action. Keep alert, and set your hope completely on the blessing which will be given you when Jesus Christ is revealed. Be obedient to God, and do not allow your lives to be shaped by those desires you had when you were still ignorant.

℣ Lord, make me know your ways.
℟ Teach me your paths.

CONCLUDING PRAYER

Lord, holy Father, faithful to your promise
you sent your Spirit
to bring together a people divided by sin.
Give us grace to foster unity and peace among men.
Through Christ our Lord.

Midday

SCRIPTURE READING 1 PET 1:15-16

Be holy in all you do, since it is the Holy One who has called you, and scripture says: Be holy, for I am holy.

℣ Your priests shall be clothed with holiness.
℟ Your faithful shall ring out their joy.

CONCLUDING PRAYER

God of power and love,
look kindly on the tasks we have begun,

and at this midday hour renew your grace within us:
make good our defects
and bring our work to that fulfilment
which accords with your will.
Through Christ our Lord.

Afternoon

SCRIPTURE READING JAS 4:7-8a, 10

Be God's true subjects; stand firm against the devil, and he will run away from you, come close to God, and he will come close to you. Humble yourselves before the Lord, and he will exalt you.

℣ The Lord looks on those who revere him.
℟ He is close to those who hope in his love.

CONCLUDING PRAYER

On the cross, Lord Jesus Christ,
you stretched out your hands for the salvation of the human race;
grant that our live and work
may be pleasing to you
and bear witness to the power of your redeeming love.
Who live and reign for ever and ever.

WEEK 1: THURSDAY

Hymn *(see p. 9)*

PSALMODY

In Advent, Christmastide and Lent the antiphons are proper.

Ant. Eastertide: Alleluia, alleluia, alleluia.
Ant. 1: Take the veil from my eyes, Lord, that I may see the wonders of your law.

PSALM 118(119):17-24 III (GIMEL)

Bless your sérvant and Í shall líve*
and obéy your wórd.

Ópen my éyes that I may sée*
the wónders of your láw.

Í am a pílgrim on the éarth;*
shów me your commánds.
My sóul is éver consúmed*
as I lóng for your decrées.

You thréaten the próud, the accúrsed,*
who túrn from your commánds.
Relíeve me from scórn and contémpt*
for I dó your wíll.

Though prínces sit plótting agáinst me*
I pónder on your rúlings.
Your wíll is mý delíght;*
your státutes are my cóunsellors.

Ant. Take the veil from my eyes, Lord, that I may see the wonders of your law.
Ant. 2: Lord, guide me in your truth.

BEGGING FOR FORGIVENESS AND SALVATION PSALM 24(25)

Our hope will not deceive us (Rom 5:5)

I

To you, O Lórd, I líft up my sóul.†
I trúst you, let me nót be disappóinted;*
do not lét my énemies tríumph.
Those who hópe in you shall nót be disappóinted,*
but only thóse who wántonly break fáith.

Lórd, make me knów your wáys.*
Lórd, téach me your páths.
Make me wálk in your trúth, and téach me:*
for yóu are Gód my sáviour.

In yóu I hópe all day lóng*
becáuse of your góodness, O Lórd.
Remémber your mércy, Lórd,*

and the lóve you have shówn from of óld.
Do not remémber the síns of my yóuth.*
In your lóve remémber mé.

The Lórd is góod and úpright.*
He shows the páth to thóse who stráy,
He guides the húmble in the ríght páth;*
He téaches his wáy to the póor.

His wáys are fáithfulness and lóve*
for those who kéep his cóvenant and láw.
Lórd, for the sáke of your náme*
forgíve my guílt; for it is gréat.

Ant. Lord, guide me in your truth.
Ant. 3: Pity me, Lord, as you see me friendless and forlorn.

II

If ányone féars the Lórd*
he will shów him the páth he should chóose.

His sóul shall líve in háppiness*
and his chíldren shall posséss the lánd.
The Lord's fríendship is for thóse who revére him;*
to thém he revéals his cóvenant.

My éyes are álways on the Lórd;*
for he réscues my féet from the snáre.
Túrn to mé and have mércy*
for Í am lónely and póor.

Relíeve the ánguish of my héart*
and sét me frée from my distréss.
Sée my afflíction and my tóil*
And táke all my síns awáy.

Sée how mány are my fóes;*
how víolent their hátred for mé.
Presérve my lífe and réscue me.*
Do not disappóint me, yóu are my réfuge.
May ínnocence and úprightness protéct me:*

for my hópe is in yóu, O Lórd.

Redeem Ísrael, O Gód,* from áll its distréss.

Ant. Pity me, Lord, as you see me friendless and forlorn.
Eastertide: Alleluia, alleluia, alleluia.

At the other Hours, the complementary psalms.

Through the Year

Before Noon

SCRIPTURE READING AMOS 4:13

He it was who formed the mountains, created the wind,
reveals his mind to man,
changes dawn to darkness,
and walks on the top of the heights of the world;
the Lord God of Sabaoth is his name.
℣ All things the Lord has made, bless the Lord.
℟ Give glory and eternal praise to him.

CONCLUDING PRAYER

Lord, who at this hour
bestowed the gift of the Holy Spirit on the apostles while they were at prayer:
grant us a share in that same grace.
Through Christ our Lord.

Midday

SCRIPTURE READING AMOS 5:8

It is he who made the Pleiades and Orion,
who turns the dusk to dawn
and the day to darkest night.
He summons the waters of the sea
and pours them over the land.
The Lord is his name.
℣ Majesty and state are his.
℟ There is power and splendour in his holy place.

CONCLUDING PRAYER

Almighty God,
you are all light,
in you there is no darkness.
Let your light shine upon us in all its radiance,
so that we may walk gladly in the way of your commandments.
Through Christ our Lord.

Afternoon

SCRIPTURE READING AMOS 9:6

He has built his high dwelling place in the heavens
and supported his vault on the earth;
he summons the waters of the sea
and pours them over the land.
The Lord is his name.
℣ The heavens proclaim the glory of God.
℟ The firmament shows forth the work of his hands.

WEEK 1: FRIDAY

Hymn *(see p. 9)*

PSALMODY

In Advent, Christmastide and Lent the antiphons are proper.

Ant. Eastertide: Alleluia, alleluia, alleluia.
Ant. 1: I will run the way of your commands, when you give me a docile heart.

PSALM 118(119):25-32 IV (DALETH)

My sóul líes in the dúst;*
by your wórd revíve me.
I decláred my wáys and you ánswered:*
téach me your státutes.

Make me grásp the wáy of your précepts*
and I will múse on your wónders.

My sóul pines awáy with gríef;*
by your wórd raise me úp.

Kéep me from the wáy of érror*
and téach me your láw.
I have chósen the wáy of trúth*
with your decrées befóre me.

I bínd myself to dó your wíll;*
Lord, dó not disappóint me.
I will rún the wáy of your commánds;*
you give fréedom to my héart.

Ant. I will run the way of your commands, when you give me a docile heart.
Ant. 2: I trust in the Lord; I have not wavered.

THE PRAYER OF CONFIDENCE OF AN INNOCENT MAN PSALM 25(26)

God has chosen us in Christ, that we may be holy and unstained (Eph 1:4)

Give júdgment for mé, O Lórd:†
for I wálk the páth of perféction.*
I trúst in the Lórd; I have not wávered.

Exámine me, Lórd, and trý me;*
O tést my héart and my mínd,
for your lóve is befóre my éyes*
and I wálk accórding to your trúth.

I néver take my pláce with líars*
and with hýpocrites I shāll not gó.
I háte the évil-doer's cómpany:*
I wíll not take my pláce with the wícked.

To prove my ínnocence I wásh my hánds*
and take my pláce aróund your áltar,
sínging a sóng of thanksgíving,*
procláiming áll your wónders.

O Lórd, I love the hóuse where you dwéll,*
the pláce where your glóry abídes.

Do not swéep me awáy with sínners,*
nor my lífe with blóodthirsty mén
in whose hánds are évil plóts,*
whose ríght hands are fílled with góld.

As for mé, I walk the páth of perféction.*
Redéem me and shów me your mércy.
My fóot stands on lével gróund:*
I will bléss the Lórd in the assémbly.

Ant. I trust in the Lord; I have not wavered.
Ant. 3: In the Lord my heart trusts, so I am sustained.

SUPPLICATION AND THANKSGIVING PSALM 27(28):1-3,6-9

Father, I give you thanks, since you have heard me (Jn 11:41)

To yóu, O Lórd, I cáll,*
my róck, héar me.
If yóu do not héed I shall becóme*
like thóse in the gráve.

Héar the vóice of my pléading*
as I cáll for hélp,
as I líft up my hánds in práyer*
to your hóly pláce.

Do not drág me awáy with the wícked,*
with the évil-dóers,
who spéak words of péace to their néighbours*
but with évil in their héarts.

Bléssed be the Lórd for he has héard*
my crý, my appéal.
The Lórd is my stréngth and my shíeld;*
in hím my heart trústs.

I was hélped, my héart rejóices*
and I práise him with my sóng.

The Lórd is the stréngth of his péople,*
a fórtress where his anóinted find hélp.

Save your péople; bless Ísrael your héritage.*
Be their shépherd and cárry them for éver.

Ant. In the Lord my heart trusts, so I am sustained.
Eastertide: Alleluia, alleluia, alleluia.

At the other Hours, the complementary psalms.

Through the Year

Before Noon

SCRIPTURE READING PHIL 2:2b-4

Have the same thoughts, sharing the same love, and being one in soul and mind. Do not do anything from selfish ambition, or from a cheap desire to boast; but be humble towards each other, never thinking you are better than others. And look out for each other's interests, not just for your own.

℣ The ways of the Lord are faithfulness and love.
℟ These are the ways of those who keep his covenant and will.

CONCLUDING PRAYER

Lord Jesus Christ,
at this hour you were led to the cross
to suffer the penalty of death
for the salvation of mankind:
in your mercy grant us pardon for our past offences
and by your power preserve us from future falls.
Who live and reign for ever and ever.

Midday

SCRIPTURE READING 2 COR 13:4

Even though it was in weakness that Christ was put to death on the cross, it is by God's power that he lives. In union with him we also are weak; but we shall live with him by God's power.

℣ My soul lies in the dust.
℟ Lord, revive me by your word.

CONCLUDING PRAYER

Lord Jesus Christ,
who at this hour
when the whole world was shrouded in darkness,
mounted the wood of the cross
as the innocent victim for our redemption,
give us always that light
which will bring us to eternal life.
Who live and reign for ever and ever.

Afternoon

SCRIPTURE READING COL 3:12-13

You are the people of God; he loved you and chose you for his own. So then, you must put on compassion, kindness, humility, gentleness, and patience. Be helpful to one another, and forgive one another, whenever any of you has a complaint against someone else. You must forgive each other in the same way that the Lord has forgiven you.

℣ The Lord is compassion and love.
℟ He is slow to anger and rich in mercy.

CONCLUDING PRAYER

Lord Jesus Christ,
who on the cross called the penitent thief into your kingdom,
in faith and trust and confessing our sins
we implore your mercy
that after our death
you will lead us rejoicing through the gates of paradise.
Who live and reign for ever and ever.

WEEK 1: SATURDAY

Hymn *(see p. 9)*

PSALMODY

In Advent, Christmastide and Lent the antiphons are proper.

Ant. Eastertide: Alleluia, alleluia, alleluia.
Ant. 1: Lead me, Lord, in the path of your commands.

PSALM 118(119):33-40 V (HE)

Téach me the demánds of your précepts*
and I will kéep them to the énd.
Tráin me to obsérve your láw,*
and kéep it with my héart.

Guíde me in the páth of your commánds;*
for thére is my delíght.
Bénd my héart to your wíll*
and nót to love of gáin.

Kéep my éyes from what is fálse:*
by your wórd, give me lífe.
Kéep the prómise you have máde*
to the sérvant who féars you.

Kéep me from the scórn I dréad,*
for your decrées are góod.
Sée, I lóng for your précepts:*
then in your jústice, give me lífe.

Ant. Lead me, Lord, in the path of your commands.
Ant. 2: Those who seek the Lord lack no blessing.

THE LORD IS THE SALVATION OF THE JUST PSALM 33(34)

You have tasted and seen that the Lord is sweet (1 Pet 2:3)

I

I will bléss the Lórd at all tímes,*

his práise álways on my líps;
in the Lórd my sóul shall make its bóast.*
The húmble shall héar and be glád.

Glórify the Lórd with mé.*
Togéther let us práise his náme.
I sóught the Lórd and he ánswered me;*
from all my térrors he sét me frée.

Lóok towards hím and be rádiant;*
let your fáces nót be abáshed.
This póor man cálled; the Lórd héard him*
and réscued him from áll his distréss.

The ángel of the Lórd is encámped*
around thóse who revére him, to réscue them.
Taste and sée that the Lórd is góod.*
He is háppy who seeks réfuge in hím.

Revére the Lórd, you his sáints.*
They lack nóthing, thóse who revére him.
Strong líons suffer wánt and go húngry*
but thóse who seek the Lórd lack no bléssing.

Ant. Those who seek the Lord lack no blessing.
Ant. 3: Let peace be all your quest and aim.

II

Cóme, chíldren, and héar me*
that I may téach you the féar of the Lórd.
Who is hé who lóngs for lífe*
and many dáys, to enjóy his prospérity?

Then kéep your tóngue from évil*
and your líps from spéaking decéit.
Turn asíde from évil and do góod;*
séek and stríve after péace.

The Lórd turns his fáce against the wícked*
to destróy their remémbrance from the éarth.
The Lórd turns his éyes to the júst*
and his éars to théir appéal.

They cáll and the Lórd héars*
and réscues them in áll their distréss.
The Lord is clóse to the brróken-héarted;*
those whose spírit is crúshed he will sáve.

Mány are the tríals of the júst man*
but from them áll the Lórd will réscue him.
He will keep guárd over áll his bónes,*
not óne of his bónes shall be brróken.

Évil brings déath to the wícked;*
those who háte the góod are dóomed.
The Lord ránsoms the sóuls of his sérvants.*
Those who híde in him shall nót be condémned.

Ant. Let peace be all your quest and aim.
Eastertide: Alleluia, alleluia, alleluia.

At the other Hours, the complementary psalms.

Through the Year

Before Noon

SCRIPTURE READING 1 KINGS 8:60-61

May all the peoples of the earth know that the Lord is God; there is no other. Let your heart therefore be wholly true to the Lord our God, walking in his statutes and keeping his commandments.

℣ You are my God, teach me your paths.
℟ Make me walk in your truth.

CONCLUDING PRAYER

Send forth the light of the Holy Spirit on us,
Lord God, almighty Father,
subject as we are to your divine majesty:
so that safe from every foe,
we may always rejoice
as we celebrate your praise.
Through Christ our Lord.

Midday

SCRIPTURE READING JER 17:9-10

The heart is more devious than any other thing,
perverse too: who can pierce its secrets?
I the Lord search to the heart,
I probe the loins,
to give each man what his conduct
and his actions deserve.
℣ From hidden faults acquit me, Lord.
℟ From presumption restrain your servant.

CONCLUDING PRAYER

Lord God,
living light of eternal love,
grant that always aglow with charity,
we may love you above all else
and our brethren for your sake,
with one and the selfsame love.
Through Christ our Lord.

Afternoon

SCRIPTURE READING WIS 7:27a;8:1

Although alone, the Wisdom of God can do all;
herself unchanging, she makes all things new.
She deploys her strength from one end of the earth to the other,
ordering all things for good.
℣ O Lord, how great are your works.
℟ How wonderful are your designs.

WEEK 2: SUNDAY

HYMN

Come, Holy Spirit, live in us
With God the Father and the Son,
And grant us your abundant grace
To sanctify and make us one.

May mind and tongue made strong in love,
Your praise throughout the world proclaim,
And may that love within our hearts
Set fire to others with its flame.

Most blessed Trinity of love
For whom the heart of man was made,
To you be praise in timeless song,
And everlasting homage paid.

PSALMODY

In Advent, Christmastide and Lent the antiphons are proper.

Ant. Eastertide: Alleluia, alleluia, alleluia.
Ant. 1: Fresh and green are the pastures where the Lord gives me repose, alleluia.

THE GOOD SHEPHERD — PSALM 22(23)

The Lamb is their king who leads them to the source of the water of life (Rev 7:17)

The Lórd is my shépherd;*
there is nóthing I shall wánt.
Frésh and gréen are the pástures*
where he gíves me repóse.
Near réstful wáters he léads me,*
to revíve my drooping spírit.

He guídes me alóng the right páth;*
he is trúe to his náme.
If I should wálk in the válley of dárkness*

no évil would I féar.
You are thére with your cróok and your stáff;*
with thése you give me cómfort.

You have prepáred a bánquet for mé*
in the síght of my fóes.
My héad you have anóinted with óil;*
my cúp is overflówing.

Surely góodness and kíndness shall fóllow me*
all the dáys of my lífe.
In the Lórd's own hóuse shall I dwéll*
for éver and éver.

Ant. Fresh and green are the pastures where the Lord gives me repose, alleluia.
Ant. 2: In Israel the name of the Lord is great, alleluia.

THANKSGIVING FOR VICTORY PSALM 75(76)

They will see the Son of Man coming on the clouds of heaven (Mt 24:30)

I

Gód is made knówn in Júdah;*
In Ísrael his náme is gréat.
He sét up his tént in Jerúsalem*
and his dwélling pláce in Síon.
It was thére he bróke the flashing árrows,*
the shíeld, the swórd, the ármour.

Yóu, O Lórd, are respléndent,*
more majéstic than the éverlasting móuntains.
The wárriors, despóiled, slept in déath;*
the hánds of the sóldiers were pówerless.
At your thréat, O Gód of Jácob,*
hórse and ríder lay stúnned.

Ant. In Israel the name of the Lord is great, alleluia.
Ant. 3: The earth in terror was still when God arose to judge, alleluia.

II

Yóu, you alóne, strike térror.*
Who shall stánd when your ánger is róused?
You úttered your séntence from the héavens;*
the éarth in térror was stíll
when Gód aróse to júdge,*
to sáve the húmble of the éarth.

Men's ánger will sérve to práise you;†
its survívors surróund you in jóy.*
Make vóws to your Gód and fulfíl them.
Let all pay tríbute to hím who strikes térror,†
who cúts short the lífe of prínces,*
who strikes térror in the kíngs of the éarth.

Ant. The earth in terror was still when God arose to judge, alleluia.
Eastertide: Alleluia, alleluia, alleluia.

At the other Hours, the complementary psalms.

Through the Year

Before Noon

SCRIPTURE READING ROM 5:1-2,5

Since we are justified by faith, let us have peace with God through our Lord Jesus Christ. Through him we have obtained access by faith to this grace in which we stand, and we rejoice in our hope of sharing the glory of God. Hope does not disappoint us, because God's love has been poured into our hearts through the Holy Spirit who has been given to us.
℣ I will sing for ever of the love of the Lord.
℟ Through all ages my mouth will proclaim his truth.

Midday

SCRIPTURE READING ROM 8:26

The Spirit helps us in our weakness; for we do not know how to pray as we ought, but the Spirit himself intercedes for us with sighs too deep for words.
℣ Lord, let my cry come before you.
℟ Teach me by your word.

Afternoon

SCRIPTURE READING 2 COR 1:21-22

It is God who gives both us and you our certainty in Christ; it is he who has anointed us, just as it is he who has put his seal on us, and given us the foretaste of his Spirit in our hearts.

℣ The Lord is my light and my help.
℟ He is the protector of my life.

The concluding prayer from the Proper of Seasons.

WEEK 2: MONDAY

Hymn *(see p. 38)*

PSALMODY

In Advent, Christmastide and Lent the antiphons are Proper.

Ant. Eastertide: Alleluia, alleluia, alleluia.
Ant. 1: Blessed are those who hear the word of God and keep it.

PSALM 118(119):41-48 VI (VAU)

Lórd, let your lóve come upón me,*
the saving hélp of your prómise.
And I shall ánswer thóse who táunt me*
for I trúst in your wórd.

Do not táke the word of trúth from my móuth*
for I trúst in your decrées.
I shall álways kéep your láw*
for éver and éver.

I shall wálk in the páth of fréedom*
for I séek your précepts.
I will spéak of your wíll before kíngs*
and nót be abáshed.

Your commánds have béen my delíght;*
thése I have lóved.

I will wórship your commánds and lóve them*
and pónder your wíll.

Ant. Blessed are those who hear the word of God and keep it.
Ant. 2: My food is to do the will of my Father.

THANKSGIVING AND REQUEST FOR HELP PSALM 39(40):2-14,17-18

You wanted no sacrifice or oblation, but you have prepared a body for me (Heb 10:5)

I

I wáited, I wáited for the Lórd†
and he stóoped down to mé;*
he héard my crý.

He dréw me from the déadly pít,*
from the míry cláy.
He sét my féet upon a róck*
and made my fóotsteps fírm.

He pút a new sóng into my móuth,*
práise of our Gód.
Mány shall sée and féar*
and shall trúst in the Lórd.

Háppy the mán who has pláced*
his trúst in the Lórd
and has nót gone óver to the rébels*
who fóllow false góds.

How mány, O Lórd my Gód,†
(are the wónders and desígns
that yóu have wórked for ús;*
you háve no équal.
Shóuld I procláim and spéak of them,*
they are móre than I can téll!

You do not ásk for sácrifice and ófferings,*
but an ópen éar.
You do not ásk for hólocaust and víctim.*

Instéad, here am Í.

In the scróll of the bóok it stands wrítten*
that Í should do your wíll.
My Gód, I delíght in your láw*
in the dépth of my héart.

Ant. My food is to do the will of my Father.
Ant. 3: Though I am wretched and poor, the Lord will take care of me.

II

Your jústice Í have procláimed*
in the gréat assémbly.
My líps I háve not séaled;*
you knów it, O Lórd.

I have not hídden your jústice in my héart*
but declared your faithful hélp.
I have not hídden your lóve and your trúth*
from the gréat assémbly.

O Lórd, you wíll not withhóld*
your compássion from mé.
Your mérciful lóve and your trúth*
will álways guárd me.

For Í am besét with évils*
too mány to be cóunted.
My síns have fállen upón me*
and my síght fáils me.
They are móre than the háirs of my héad*
and my héart sínks.

O Lórd, cóme to my réscue,*
Lord, cóme to my áid.

O lét there be rejóicing and gládness*
for áll who séek you.
Let them éver say: 'The Lórd is gréat',*
who lóve your saving hélp.

As for mé, wrétched and póor,*
the Lórd thinks of mé.
Yóu are my réscuer, my hélp,*
O Gód, do not deláy.

Ant. Though I am wretched and poor, the Lord will take care of me.
Eastertide: Alleluia, alleluia, alleluia.

At the other Hours, the complementary psalms.

Through the Year

Before Noon

SCRIPTURE READING JER 31:33

This is the covenant I will make with the House of Israel when those days arrive – it is the Lord who speaks. Deep within them I will plant my Law, writing it on their hearts. Then I will be their God and they shall be my people.

℣ Put a steadfast heart within me, O God.
℟ Do not cast me away from your presence.

CONCLUDING PRAYER

Father, Creator of all that is good,
you have called men to work in your world,
and by their co-operation to better the condition of mankind.
Grant that we may always work together as children of your family,
and love all men as our brethren.
Through Christ our Lord.

Midday

SCRIPTURE READING JER 32:40

I will make an everlasting covenant with them; I will not cease in my efforts for their good, and I will put respect for me into their hearts, so that they turn from me no more.

℣ God is my glory and my salvation.
℟ He is my refuge.

CONCLUDING PRAYER

God, Lord and master of the vineyard,
you allot us our tasks
and determine the just rewards of our labours.
Help us to bear the burden of the day
and accept your will in all things without complaint.
Through Christ our Lord.

Afternoon

SCRIPTURE READING EZEK 34:31

You, my sheep, are the flock of men I shall pasture, and I am your God – it is the Lord God who speaks.

℣ The Lord is my shepherd; there is nothing I shall want.
℟ Fresh and green are the pastures where he gives me repose.

CONCLUDING PRAYER

God our Father,
you are calling us to prayer,
at that same hour
when the apostles went up to the temple.
Grant that the prayer we offer with sincere hearts
in the name of Jesus,
may bring salvation to all who call upon that holy Name.
Through Christ our Lord.

WEEK 2: TUESDAY

Hymn *(see p. 38)*

PSALMODY

In Advent, Christmastide and Lent the antiphons are proper.

Ant. Eastertide: Alleluia, alleluia, alleluia.
Ant 1: I have kept your precepts in the land of my exile.

PSALM 118(119):49-56 VII (ZAIN)

Remémber your wórd to your sérvant*

by whích you gave me hópe.
Thís is my cómfort in sórrow*
that your prómise gives me lífe.

Though the próud may útterly deríde me*
I kéep to your láw.
I remémber your decrées of óld*
and thése, Lord, consóle me.

I am séized with indignátion at the wícked*
who forsáke your láw.
Your commánd has becóme my sóng*
in the lánd of éxile.

I thínk of your náme in the níght-time*
and I kéep your láw.
Thís has béen my bléssing,*
the kéeping of your précepts.

Ant. I have kept your precepts in the land of my exile.
Ant. 2: The Lord will deliver his people from bondage and we will rejoice.

THE FOOLISHNESS OF SINNERS PSALM 52(53)

All have sinned and forfeited the glory of God (Rom 3:23)

The fóol has sáid in his héart:*
'There is no Gód abóve.'
Their déeds are corrúpt, depráved;*
not a góod man is léft.

Gód looks dówn from héaven*
on the sóns of mén,
to sée if ány are wíse,*
if ány seek Gód.

Áll have left the ríght páth;*
depráved, every óne.
There is nót a góod man léft,*
nó, not even óne.

Will the évil-doers nót understánd?*
They éat up my péople
as thoúgh they were éating bréad;*
they néver pray to Gód.

Sée how they trémble with féar*
without cáuse for féar:
for Gód scatters the bónes of the wícked.*
They are shámed, God rejécts them.

O that Ísrael's salvátion might cóme from Síon!†
When Gód delívers his péople from bóndage,*
then Jácob will be glád and Ísrael rejóice.

Ant. The Lord will deliver his people from bondage and we will rejoice.
Ant. 3: I have God for my help. The Lord upholds my life.

CRY FOR GOD'S HELP PSALM 53(54):1-6,8-9

The prophet prays in the name of the Lord to be freed from the evil of those who persecute him (Cassian).

O Gód, sáve me by your náme;*
by your pówer, uphóld my cáuse.
O Gód, héar my práyer;*
listén to the wórds of my móuth.

For próud men have rísen agáinst me,†
rúthless men séek my lífe.*
They háve no regárd for Gód.
But Í have Gód for my hélp.*
The Lórd uphólds my lífe.

I will sácrifice to yóu with willing héart*
and práise your náme for it is góod:
for you have réscued me from áll my distréss*
and my éyes have seen the dównfall of my fóes.

Ant. I have God for my help. The Lord upholds my life.
Eastertide: Alleluia, alleluia, alleluia.

At the other Hours, the complementary psalms.

Through the Year

Before Noon

SCRIPTURE READING 1 COR 12:4-6

There is a variety of gifts but always the same Spirit; there are all sorts of service to be done, but always the same Lord; working in all sorts of different ways in different people, it is the same God who is working in all of them.

℣ The help of God is near for those who fear him.
℟ His glory will dwell in our land.

CONCLUDING PRAYER

Almighty ever-living God.
who at this hour sent down your Holy Spirit on the apostles,
send forth that same Spirit of love into our hearts
so that we may bear faithful witness to you,
before all mankind.
Through Christ our Lord.

Midday

SCRIPTURE READING 1 COR 12:12-13

Just as a human body, though it is made up of many parts, is a single unit because all these parts, though many, make one body, so it is with Christ. In the one Spirit we were all baptized, Jews as well as Greeks, slaves as well as citizens, and one Spirit was given to us all to drink.

℣ Holy Father, keep us true to your name.
℟ Grant that we may all be one.

CONCLUDING PRAYER

Almighty God,
who revealed to Peter your plan for the salvation of all men,
grant that our work may be acceptable to you,
and that, by your grace, it may further your loving purpose of redemption.
Through Christ our Lord.

Afternoon

SCRIPTURE READING 1 COR 12:24b,25-26

God has established a harmony in the body, giving special honour to that which needed it most. There was to be no want of unity in the body; all the different parts of it were to make each other's welfare their common care. If one part is suffering, all the rest suffer with it; if one part is treated with honour, all the rest find pleasure in it.

℣ Lord, our God, gather us from among the nations.
℟ That we may give praise to your holy name.

CONCLUDING PRAYER

Almighty God,
we recall how you sent your angel to the centurion Cornelius
to show him the way of salvation.
Open our hearts to work more zealously
for the salvation of the world,
so that your Church
may bring us and all men into your presence.
Through Christ our Lord.

WEEK 2: WEDNESDAY

Hymn *(see p. 38)*

PSALMODY

In Advent, Christmastide and Lent the antiphons are proper.

Ant. Eastertide: Alleluia, alleluia, alleluia.
Ant. 1: I have pondered over my ways and returned to your will.

PSALM 118(119):57-64 VIII (HETH)

My párt, I have resólved, O Lórd,*
is to obéy your wórd.
With all my héart I implóre your fávour;*
show the mércy of your prómise.

I have póndered óver my wáys*
and retúrned to your wîll.
I made háste and díd not deláy*
to obéy your commánds.

Though the néts of the wícked ensnáred me*
I remémbered your láw.
At mídnight I will ríse and thánk you*
for your júst decrées.

I am a fríend of áll who revére you,*
who obéy your précepts.
Lórd, your lóve fills the eárth.*
Téach me your commánds.

Ant. I have pondered over my ways and returned to your will.
Ant. 2: Trembling and fear fall upon me; turn to me, Lord, and listen to my cry.

AGAINST FALSE FRIENDS PSALM 54(55):2-15,17-24

Jesus began to feel a sudden fear and great distress (Mk 14:33)

I

O Gód, lísten to my práyer,*
do not híde from my pléading,
atténd to mé and replý;*
with my cáres, I cannot rést.

I trémble at the shóuts of the fóe,*
at the críes of the wícked;
for they bríng down évil upón me.*
They assáil me with fúry.

My héart is strícken withín me,*
death's térror is ón me,
trémbling and féar fall upón me*
and hórror overwhélms me.

Ó that I had wíngs like a dóve*
to fly awáy and be at rést.

Só I would escápe far awáy*
and take réfuge in the désert.

I would hásten to fínd a shélter*
from the ráging wínd,
from the destrúctive stórm, O Lórd,*
and from their plótting tóngues.

For Í can see nóthing but víolence*
and strífe in the cíty.
Níght and dáy they patról*
hígh on the city wálls.

It is fúll of wíckedness and évil;*
it is fúll of sín.
Its stréets are néver frée*
from týranny and decéit.

Ant. Trembling and fear fall upon me; turn to me, Lord, and listen to my cry.
Ant. 3: I will cry to God and the Lord will save me.

II

If thís had been dóne by an énemy*
I could béar his táunts.
If a ríval had rísen agáinst me,*
I could híde from hím.

But it is yóu, my ówn compánion,*
my íntimate fríend!
How clóse was the fríendship betwéen us.†
We wálked togéther in hármony*
in the hóuse of Gód.

As for mé, I will crý to Gód*
and the Lórd will sáve me.
Évening, mórning and at nóon*
I will crý and lamént.

He will delíver my sóul in péace*
in the attáck agáinst me:

for thóse who fíght me are mány,*
but he héars my vóice.

Gód will héar and will húmble them,*
the etérnal júdge:
for they wíll not aménd their wáys.*
They have no féar of Gód.

The tráitor has túrned against his fríends;*
he has bróken his wórd.
His spéech is sófter than bútter,*
but wár is in his héart.
His wórds are smóother than óil,*
but they are náked swórds.

Entrúst your cáres to the Lórd*
and hé will suppórt you.
Hé will néver allów*
the júst man to stúmble.

But yóu, O Gód, will bring them dówn*
to the pít of déath.
Decéitful and blóodthirsty mén†
(shall not líve half their dáys.*
O Lórd, I will trúst in yóu.)

Ant. I will cry to God and the Lord will save me.
Eastertide: Alleluia, alleluia, alleluia.

At the other Hours, the complementary psalms.

Before Noon

SCRIPTURE READING DEUT 1:16-17a

At that same time I told your judges: You must give your brothers a fair hearing and see justice done between a man and his brother or the stranger who lives with him. You must be impartial in judgment and give an equal hearing to small and great alike. Do not be afraid of any man, for the judgment is God's.
℣ The Lord is just, he loves just ways.
℟ The upright shall see his face.

CONCLUDING PRAYER

Lord, holy Father, faithful to your promise
you sent your Spirit
to bring together a people divided by sin.
Give us grace to foster unity and peace among men.
Through Christ our Lord.

Midday

SCRIPTURE READING IS 55:8-9

My thoughts are not your thoughts,
my ways not your ways – it is the Lord who speaks.
Yes, the heavens are as high above the earth
as my ways are above your ways,
my thoughts above your thoughts.
℣ Lord God Almighty, who is your equal?
℟ You are mighty, Lord, and truth is your garment.

CONCLUDING PRAYER

God of power and love,
look kindly on the tasks we have begun,
and at this midday hour renew your grace within us:
make good our defects
and bring our work to that fulfilment
which accords with your will.
Through Christ our Lord.

Afternoon

SCRIPTURE READING 1 SAM 16:7b

God does not see as man sees; man looks at appearances but the Lord looks at the heart.
℣ Search me, O God, and know my heart.
℟ Lead me in the path of eternal life.

CONCLUDING PRAYER

On the cross, Lord Jesus Christ,
you stretched out your hands for the salvation of the human race;
grant that our life and work
may be pleasing to you

and bear witness to the power of your redeeming love.
Who live and reign for ever and ever.

WEEK 2: THURSDAY

Hymn *(see p. 38)*

PSALMODY

In Advent, Christmastide and Lent the antiphons are proper.

Ant. Eastertide: Alleluia, alleluia, alleluia.
Ant. 1: The law from your mouth means more to me than silver and gold.

PSALM 118(119):65-72 IX (TETH)

Lórd, you have been góod to your sérvant*
accórding to your wórd.
Téach me discérnment and knówledge*
for I trúst in your commánds.

Befóre I was afflícted I stráyed*
but nów I keep your wórd.
You are góod and your déeds are góod;*
téach me your commándments.

Though próud men sméar me with líes*
yet I kéep your précepts.
Their mínds are clósed to góod*
but your láw is my delíght.

It was góod for mé to be afflícted,*
to léarn your wíll.
The láw from your móuth means móre to me*
than sílver and góld.

Ant. The law from your mouth means more to me than silver and gold.
Ant. 2: In God I trust; I shall not fear what mortal man can do to me.

CONFIDENCE IN THE WORD OF THE LORD PSALM 55(56):2-7,9-14

Christ is shown suffering (St Jerome)

Have mércy on me, Gód, men crúsh me;*
they fíght me all day lóng and oppréss me.
My fóes crúsh me all day lóng,*
for mány fight próudly agáinst me.

When I féar, I will trúst in yóu,*
in Gód whose wórd I práise.
In God I trúst, I sháll not féar:*
whát can mortal mán do to mé?

All day lóng they distórt my wórds,*
áll their thóught is to hárm me.
They bánd togéther in ámbush,*
track me dówn and séek my lífe.

You have képt an accóunt of my wánderings;†
you have képt a récord of my téars;*
áre they not wrítten in your bóok?
Then my fóes will be pút to flíght†
on the dáy that I cáll to yóu.*

This I knów, that Gód is on my síde.
In Gód, whose wórd I práise,*
in the Lórd, whose wórd I práise,
in Gód I trúst; I shall not féar:*
whát can mortal mán do to mé?

I am bóund by thc vóws I have máde you.*
O Gód, I will óffer you práise
for you réscued my sóul from déath,*
you képt my féet from stúmbling
that I may wálk in the présence of Gód*
and enjóy the líght of the líving.

Ant. In God I trust; I shall not fear what mortal man can do to me.
Ant. 3: Your merciful love reaches to the heavens, Lord.

MORNING PRAYER IN TIME OF AFFLICTION PSALM 56(57)

This psalm tells of the passion of the Lord (St Augustine)

Have mércy on me, Gód, have mércy*
for in yóu my sóul has taken réfuge.
In the shádow of your wíngs I take réfuge*
till the stórms of destrúction pass bý.

I cáll to Gód the Most Hígh,*
to Gód who has álways been my hélp.
May he sénd from héaven and sáve me†
(and sháme thóse who assáil me.*
May Gód send his trúth and his lóve.

My sóul lies dówn among líons,*
who would devóur the sóns of mén.
Their téeth are spéars and árrows,*
their tóngue a shárpened swórd.

O Gód, aríse above the héavens;*
may your glóry shine on eárth!

They láid a snáre for my stéps,*
my sóul was bowed dówn.
They dúg a pít in my páth*
but féll in it themsélves.

My héart is réady, O Gód,†
my héart is réady.*
I will síng, I will síng your práise.
Awáke my sóul,†
awáke lýre and hárp,*
I will awáke the dáwn.

I will thánk you Lórd among the péoples,*
among the nátions I will práise you
for your lóve réaches to the héavens*
and your trúth to the skíes.

O Gód, aríse above the héavens;*
may your glóry shine on eárth!

Ant. Your merciful love reaches to the heavens, Lord.
Eastertide: Alleluia, alleluia, alleluia.
At the other Hours, the complementary psalms.

Through the Year

Before Noon

SCRIPTURE READING GAL 5:13-14

My brothers, you were called, as you know, to liberty; but be careful, or this liberty will provide an opening for self-indulgence. Serve one another, rather, in works of love, since the whole of the Law is summarized in a single command: Love your neighbour as yourself.

℣ I will run in the way of your commands, Lord.
℟ You give freedom to my heart.

CONCLUDING PRAYER

Lord, who at this hour
bestowed the gift of the Holy Spirit on the apostles while they were at prayer:
grant us a share in that same grace.
Through Christ our Lord.

Midday

SCRIPTURE READING GAL 5:16-17

Learn to live and move in the spirit; then there is no danger of your giving way to the impulses of corrupt nature. The impulses of nature and the impulses of the spirit are at war with one another; either is clean contrary to the other, and that is why you cannot do all that your will approves.

℣ Lord, you are good and your ways are good.
℟ Teach me your commandments.

CONCLUDING PRAYER

Almighty God,
you are all light,
in you there is no darkness.
Let your light shine upon us in all its radiance,
so that we may walk gladly in the way of your commandments.
Through Christ our Lord.

Afternoon

SCRIPTURE READING GAL 5:22,23a,25

The spirit yields a harvest of love, joy, peace, patience, kindness, generosity, forbearance, gentleness, faith, courtesy, temperateness, purity. Since we live by the spirit, let the spirit be our rule of life.

℣ Lord, make me know the way I should walk.
℟ Let your good Spirit guide me along the right way.

CONCLUDING PRAYER

Lord, in answer to our prayer
give us patience in suffering hardships
after the example of your Only-begotten Son,
who lives and reigns for ever and ever.

WEEK 2: FRIDAY

Hymn *(see p. 38)*

PSALMODY

In Advent, Christmastide and Lent the antiphons are proper.

Ant. Eastertide: Alleluia, alleluia, alleluia.
Ant. 1: Let your love be ready to console me according to your promise.

PSALM 118(119):73-80 X(YOD)

It was yóur hands that máde me and sháped me;*
help me to léarn your commánds.
Your fáithful will sée me and rejóice*
for I trúst in your wórd.

Lord, I knów that your decrées are ríght,*
that you afflícted me jústly.
Let your lóve be réady to consóle me*
by your prómise to your sérvant.

Let your lóve cóme and I shall líve*
for your láw is my delíght.

Shame the próud who hárm me with líes*
while I pónder your précepts.

Let your fáithful túrn to mé,*
those who knów your wíll.
Let my héart be blámeless in obéying you*
lést I be ashámed.

Ant. Let your love be ready to console me according to your promise.
Ant. 2: Protect me, my God, from those who attack me.

PRAYER FOR PROTECTION AGAINST ASSAILANTS — PSALM 58(59):2-5,10-11,17-18

Let these words of the Saviour teach all men to look to his Father like dutiful sons (Eusebius of Caesarea).

Réscue me, Gód, from my fóes;*
protéct me from thóse who attáck me.
O réscue me from thóse who do évil*
and sáve me from blóod-thirsty mén.

See, they líe in wáit for my lífe;*
powerful mén band togéther agáinst me.
For no offénce, no sín of mine, Lórd,†
for no guílt of mine they rúsh to take their stánd.*
Awáke, come to my áid and sée!

O my Stréngth, it is yóu to whom I túrn,†
for yóu, O Gód, are my strónghold,*
the Gód who shóws me lóve.

O Gód, cóme to my áid*
and let me lóok in tríumph on my fóes.

As for mé, I will síng of your stréngth*
and each mórning accláim your lóve
for yóu have béen my strónghold,*
a réfuge in the dáy of my distréss.

O my Stréngth, it is yóu to whom I túrn,†
for yóu, O Gód, are my strónghold,*
the Gód who shóws me lóve.

Ant. Protect me, my God, from those who attack me.
Ant. 3: Blessed is the man whom God corrects; though he may hurt us he is also our healer.

PRAYER IN TIME OF DISTRESS AND FAILURE PSALM 59(60)

In the world you will have trouble, but be brave: I have overcome the world (Jn 16:33).

O Gód, you have rejécted us and bróken us.*
Yóu have been ángry; come báck to us.

You have máde the earth quáke, torn it ópen.*
Repáir what is sháttered for it swáys.
You have inflícted hárdships on your péople*
and máde us drink a wíne that dázed us.

You have gíven those who féar you a sígnal*
to flée from the énemy's bów.
O cóme and delíver your fríends,*
hélp with your ríght hand and replý.

From his hóly place Gód has made this prómise;†
'I will tríumph and divíde the land of Shéchem,*
I will méasure out the válley of Súccoth.

Gílead is míne and Manásseh,†
Éphraim I táke for my hélmet,*
Júdah for my commánder's stáff.

Móab I will úse for my wáshbowl;†
on Édom I will plánt my shóe.*
Over the Phílistines I will shóut in tríumph.'

But who will léad me to cónquer the fórtress?*
Who will bríng me face to fáce with Édom?
Will you útterly rejéct us, O Gód,*
and no lónger márch with our ármies?

Give us hélp agáinst the fóe:*
for the hélp of mán is váin.
With Gód wé shall do brávely*
and hé will trámple down our fóes.

Ant. Blessed is the man whom God corrects; though he may hurt us he is also our healer.
Eastertide: Alleluia, alleluia, alleluia.

At the other Hours, the complementary psalms from Series II and III.

Through the Year

Before Noon

SCRIPTURE READING DEUT 1:31b

The Lord carried you, as a man carries his child, all along the road you travelled.
℣ Uphold me by your promise, Lord, and I shall live.
℟ Let my hopes not be in vain.

CONCLUDING PRAYER

Lord Jesus Christ,
at this hour you were led to the cross
to suffer the penalty of death
for the salvation of mankind:
in your mercy grant us pardon for our past offences
and by your power preserve us from future falls.
Who live and reign for ever and ever.

Midday

SCRIPTURE READING BAR 4:28-29

As by your will you first strayed away from God, so now turn back and search for him ten times as hard; for as he brought down those disasters on you, so will he rescue you and give you eternal joy.
℣ With the Lord there is mercy.
℟ With him there is fulness of redemption.

CONCLUDING PRAYER

Lord Jesus Christ,
who at this hour
when the whole world was shrouded in darkness
mounted the wood of the cross
as the innocent victim for our redemption,
give us always that light

which will bring us to eternal life.
Who live and reign for ever and ever.

Afternoon

SCRIPTURE READING WIS 1:13-15

Death was never of God's fashioning; not for his pleasure does life cease to be; what meant his creation, but that all created things should have being? No breed has he created on earth but for its thriving; none carries in itself the seeds of its own destruction. Think not that mortality bears sway on earth; no end nor term is fixed to a life well lived.
℣ The Lord has kept my soul from death.
℟ I will walk in his presence in the land of the living.

CONCLUDING PRAYER

Lord Jesus Christ,
who on the cross called the penitent thief into your kingdom,
in faith and trust and confessing our sins
we implore your mercy
that after our death
you will lead us rejoicing through the gates of paradise.
Who live and reign for ever and ever.

WEEK 2: SATURDAY

Hymn *(see p. 38)*

PSALMODY

In Advent, Christmastide and Lent the antiphons are proper.

Ant. Eastertide: Alleluia, alleluia, alleluia.
Ant. 1: Heaven and earth will pass away, but my words will not pass away, says the Lord.

PSALM 118(119):81-88 XI (CAPH)

I yéarn for your sáving hélp;*
I hópe in your wórd.

My éyes yéarn to see your prómise.*
Whén will you consóle me?

Though párched and exháusted with wáiting*
I have not forgótten your commánds.
How lóng must your sérvant súffer?*
When will you júdge my fóes?

For mé the próud have dug pítfalls,*
agáinst your láw.
Your commánds are all trúe; then hélp me*
when líes oppréss me.

They álmost made an énd of me on éarth*
but I képt your précepts.
Becáuse of your lóve give me lífe*
and Í will do your wíll.

Ant. Heaven and earth will pass away, but my words will not pass away, says the Lord.
Ant. 2: You, Lord, have been my refuge, a tower of strength against the foe.

PRAYER OF AN EXILE — PSALM 60(61)

The prayer of a just man who looks to the things which are eternal (St Hilary)

O Gód, héar my crý!*
Lísten to my práyer!
From the énd of the eárth I cáll:*
my héart is fáint.

On the róck too hígh for me to réach*
sét me on hígh,
O yóu who have béen my réfuge,*
my tówer against the fóe.

Let me dwéll in your tént for éver*
and híde in the shélter of your wíngs.
For yóu, O Gód, hear my práyer,*
grant me the héritage of thóse who féar you.

May you léngthen the lífe of the kíng:*
may his yéars cover mány generátions.
May he éver sit enthróned before Gód:*
bid lóve and trúth be his protéction.

So I will álways práise your náme*
and dáy after dáy fulfil my vóws.

Ant. You, Lord, have been my refuge, a tower of strength against the foe.
Ant. 3: Lord, guard my life from dread of the foe.

PRAYER AGAINST ENEMIES PSALM 63(64)

This psalm in particular invites us to think about the passion of the Lord (St Augustine)

Hear my vóice, O Gód, as I compláin,*
guard my lífe from dréad of the fóe.
Híde me from the bánd of the wícked,*
from the thróng of thóse who do évil.

They shárpen their tóngues like swórds;*
they áim bitter wórds like árrows
to shóot at the ínnocent from ámbush,*
shóoting súddenly and récklessly.

They schéme their évil cóurse;*
they conspíre to lay sécret snáres.
They sáy: 'Whó will sée us?*
Whó can séarch out our crímes?'

He will séarch who séarches the mínd*
and knóws the dépths of the héart.
Gód has shót them with his árrow*
and déalt them súdden wóunds.
Their ówn tongue has brought them to rúin*
and áll who sée them móck.

Thén will áll men féar;†
they will téll what Gód has dóne.*
They will únderstánd God's déeds.

The júst will rejóice in the Lórd†
and flý to hím for réfuge.*
All the úpright héarts will glóry.

Ant. Lord, guard my life from dread of the foe.
Eastertide: Alleluia, alleluia, alleluia.

At the other Hours, the complementary psalms.

Through the Year

Before Noon

SCRIPTURE READING DEUT 8:5b-6

As a man disciplines his son, the Lord your God disciplines you. So you shall keep the commandments of the Lord your God, by walking in his ways and by fearing him.

℣ The fear of the Lord is holy, abiding for ever.
℟ The decrees of the Lord are truth and all of them just.

CONCLUDING PRAYER

Send forth the light of the holy Spirit on us,
Lord God, almighty Father.
subject as we are to your divine majesty:
so that safe from every foe,
we may always rejoice
as we celebrate your praise.
Through Christ our Lord.

Midday

SCRIPTURE READING 1 KINGS 2:2b-3

Be strong and show yourself a man. Observe the injunctions of the Lord your God, following his ways and keeping his laws, his commandments, his customs and his decrees, that so you may be successful in all you do and undertake.

℣ Guide me in the way of your commands, Lord.
℟ For in them is my delight.

CONCLUDING PRAYER

Lord God,
living light of eternal love,
grant that always aglow with charity,
we may love you above all else
and our brethren for your sake,
with one and the selfsame love.
Through Christ our Lord.

Afternoon

SCRIPTURE READING JER 6:16

Halt at the cross-roads, look well, and ask yourselves which path it was that stood you in good stead long ago. That path follow, and you shall find rest for your souls.

℣ Your will is my portion for ever.
℟ For in it my heart finds joy.

CONCLUDING PRAYER

Give us perfect peace, Lord,
so that we may delight in serving you
all the days of our life,
and at the last, with our Lady's help,
come safely to your presence.
Through Christ our Lord.

WEEK 3: SUNDAY

HYMN

Lord God and Maker of all things,
Creation is upheld by you.
While all must change and know decay,
You are unchanging, always new.

You are man's solace and his shield,
His Rock secure on which to build,
You are the spirit's tranquil home,
In you alone is hope fulfilled.

To God the Father and the Son
And Holy Spirit render praise,
Blest Trinity, from age to age,
The strength of all our living days.

PSALMODY

In Advent, Christmastide and Lent the antiphons are proper.

Ant. Eastertide: Alleluia, alleluia, alleluia.
Ant. 1: I called to the Lord in my distress, and he heard me, alleluia.

SONG OF REJOICING AND SALVATION — PSALM 117(118)

This is the stone which was rejected by you builders, but which has become the cornerstone (Acts 4:11)

I

Give thánks to the Lórd for he is góod,*
for his lóve endures for éver.

Let the sóns of Ísrael sáy:*
'His lóve endures for éver.'
Let the sóns of Áaron sáy:*
'His lóve endures for éver.'
Let thóse who fear the Lórd sáy:*
'His lóve endures for éver.'

I cálled to the Lórd in my distréss;*
he ánswered and fréed me.
The Lórd is at my síde; I do not féar.*
What can mán do agáinst me?
The Lórd is at my síde as my hélper:*
I shall look dówn on my fóes.

It is bétter to take réfuge in the Lórd*
than to trúst in mén:
it is bétter to take réfuge in the Lórd*
than to trúst in prínces.

Ant. I called to the Lord in my distress, and he heard me, alleluia.
Ant. 2: The Lord's right hand has raised me up, alleluia.

II

The nátions áll encómpassed me;*
in the Lórd's name I crúshed them.
They cómpassed me, cómpassed me abóut;*
in the Lórd's name I crúshed them.
They cómpassed me abóut like bées;†
they blázed like a fíre among thórns.*
In the Lórd's name I crúshed them.

I was hárd-préssed and was fálling*
but the Lórd came to hélp me.
The Lórd is my strength and my sóng;*
hé is my sáviour.
There are shóuts of jóy and víctory*
in the ténts of the júst.

The Lórd's right hánd has tríumphed;*
his ríght hand ráised me.
The Lórd's right hánd has tríumphed;†
I shall not díe, I shall líve*
and recóunt his déeds.
I was púnished, I was púnished by the Lórd,*
but nót doomed to díe.

Ant. The Lord's right hand has raised me up, alleluia.
Ant. 3: The Lord God is our light, alleluia.

III

Ópen to mé the gates of hóliness:*
I will énter and give thánks.
Thís is the Lórd's own gáte*
where the júst may énter.
I will thánk you for yóu have ánswered*
and yóu are my sáviour.

The stóne which the buílders rejécted*
has becóme the córner stone.
Thís is the wórk of the Lórd,*
a márvel in our éyes.
Thís day was máde by the Lórd;*
we rejóice and are glád.

O Lórd, gránt us salvátion;*
O Lórd, grant succéss.
Bléssed in the náme of the Lórd*
is hé who cómes.
We bléss you from the hóuse of the Lórd;*
the Lord Gód is our líght.

Go fórward in procéssion with bránches*
éven to the áltar.
Yóu are my Gód, I thánk you.*
My Gód, I práise you.
Give thánks to the Lórd for he is góod;*
for his lóve endures for éver.

Ant. The Lord God is our light, alleluia.
Eastertide: Alleluia, alleluia, alleluia.

At the other Hours, the complementary psalms.

Through the Year

Before Noon

SCRIPTURE READING ROM 8:15-16

You did not receive the spirit of slavery to fall back into fear, but you have received the spirit of sonship. When we cry, Abba Father! it is the

Spirit himself bearing witness with our spirit that we are children of God.
℣ With you, O Lord, is the source of life.
℟ It is your light that enlightens us.

Midday

SCRIPTURE READING ROM 8:22-23

From the beginning till now the entire creation, as we know, has been groaning in one great act of giving birth; and not only creation, but all of us who possess the first-fruits of the Spirit, we too groan inwardly as we wait for adoptive sonship and for our bodies to be set free.
℣ Bless the Lord, my soul.
℟ It is he who redeems your life from the grave.

Afternoon

SCRIPTURE READING 2 TIM 1:9

God has saved us and called us to be holy – not because of anything we ourselves have done but for his own purpose and by his own grace. This grace has already been granted to us, in Christ Jesus, before the beginning of time.
℣ The Lord led them safely with nothing to fear.
℟ He brought them to his holy land.

The concluding prayer from the Proper of Seasons.

WEEK 3: MONDAY

Hymn *(see p. 67)*

PSALMODY

In Advent, Christmastide and Lent the antiphons are proper.

Ant. Eastertide: Alleluia, alleluia, alleluia.
Ant. 1: I seek your precepts, Lord, for with them you give me life.

MEDITATION ON THE WORD OF GOD IN THE LAW
PSALM 118(119):89-96 XII (LAMED)

This is my commandment, that you love each other as I have loved you (Jn 13:34)

Your wórd, O Lórd, for éver*
stands fírm in the héavens:
your trúth lasts from áge to áge,*
like the éarth you créated.

By your decrée it endúres to this dáy;*
for áll things sérve you.
Had your láw not béen my delíght*
I would have díed in my afflíction.

I will néver forgét your précepts*
for with thém you give me lífe.
Sáve me, for Í am yoúrs*
since I séek your précepts.

Though the wícked lie in wáit to destróy me*
yet I pónder on your wíll.
I have séen that all perféction has an énd*
but your commánd is bóundless.

Ant. I seek your precepts, Lord, for with them you give me life.
Ant. 2: O Lord, you have been my hope since my youth.

LORD, YOU ARE MY HOPE SINCE MY YOUTH PSALM 70(71)

Have hope and rejoice, show patience in times of trial (Rom 12:12)

I

In yóu, O Lórd, I take réfuge;*
let me néver be pút to sháme.
In your jústice réscue me, frée me:*
pay héed to mé and sáve me.

Be a róck where Í can take réfuge,†
a míghty strónghold to sáve me;*
for yóu are my róck, my strónghold.

Frée me from the hánd of the wícked,*
from the gríp of the unjúst, of the oppréssor.

It is yóu, O Lórd, who are my hópe,*
my trúst, O Lórd, since my yóuth.
On yóu I have léaned from my bírth,†
from my móther's womb yóu have been my hélp.*
My hópe has álways been in yóu.

My fáte has filled mány with áwe*
but yóu are my stróng réfuge.
My líps are fílled with your práise,*
with your glóry áll the day lóng.
Do not rejéct me nów that I am óld;*
when my stréngth fails dó not forsáke me.

For my énemies are spéaking abóut me;*
those who wátch me take cóunsel togéther.
They say: 'Gód has forsáken him; fóllow him,*
séize him; there is nó one to sáve him.'
O Gód, do not stáy far óff:*
my Gód, make háste to hélp me!

Let thém be put to sháme and destróyed,*
all thóse who seek my lífe.
Let them be cóvered with sháme and confúsion,*
all thóse who seek to hárm me.

Ant. O Lord, you have been my hope since my youth.
Ant. 3. When I grow old do not forsake me, O God.

II

But as for mé, I will álways hópe*
and práise you móre and móre.
My líps will téll of your jústice†
and dáy by dáy of your hélp*
though Í can néver tell it áll.

I will decláre the Lórd's mighty déeds*
procláiming your jústice, yours alóne.
O Gód, you have táught me from my yóuth*
and I procláim your wónders still.

Nów that I am óld and grey-héaded,*
dó not forsáke me, Gód.
Let me téll of your pówer to all áges,*
praise your stréngth and jústice to the skíes,
tell of yóu who have wórked such wónders.*
O Gód, whó is líke you?

You have búrdened me with bítter tróubles*
but you will gíve me báck my life.
You will ráise me from the dépths of the éarth;*
you will exált me and consóle me agáin.

So I will gíve you thánks on the lýre*
for your fáithful lóve, my Gód.
To yóu will I síng with the hárp*
to yóu, the Hóly One of Ísrael.
When I síng to you my líps shall rejóice*
and my sóul, which yóu have redéemed.

And áll the day lóng my tóngue*
shall téll the tále of your jústice.
For théy are put to sháme and disgráced,*
all thóse who séek to hárm me.

Ant. When I grow old do not forsake me, O God.
Eastertide: Alleluia, alleluia, alleluia.

At the other Hours, the complementary psalms from Series I and III.

Through the Year

Before Noon

SCRIPTURE READING 2 COR 13:11

In the meantime, brothers, we wish you happiness; try to grow perfect; help one another. Be united; live in peace, and the God of love and peace will be with you.

℣ The Lord turns his eyes to the just.
℟ He gives ear to their appeal.

CONCLUDING PRAYER

Father, creator of all that is good,
you have called men to work in your world,
and by their co-operation to better the condition of mankind.
Grant that we may always work together as children of your family,
and love all men as our brethren.
Through Christ our Lord.

Midday

SCRIPTURE READING ROM 6:22

Now that you have been set free from sin and have become slaves of God, the return you get is sanctification and its end, eternal life.

℣ Lord, we know that you will restore our life again.
℟ Then your people will rejoice in you.

CONCLUDING PRAYER

God, Lord and master of the vineyard,
you allot us our tasks
and determine the just rewards of our labours.
Help us to bear the burden of the day
and accept your will in all things without complaint.
Through Christ our Lord.

Afternoon

SCRIPTURE READING COL 1:21-22

At one time you were far away from God and were his enemies because of the evil things you did and thought. But now, by means of the physical death of his Son, God has made you his friends, in order to bring you, holy, pure, and faultless, into his presence.

℣ Sing to the Lord, you, his saints.
℟ Remember his holiness and give praise.

CONCLUDING PRAYER

God our Father,
you are calling us to prayer,
at that same hour
when the apostles went up to the temple.
Grant that the prayer we offer with sincere hearts

in the name of Jesus,
may bring salvation to all who call upon that holy Name.
Through Christ our Lord.

WEEK 3: TUESDAY

Hymn *(see p. 67)*

PSALMODY

In Advent, Christmastide and Lent the antiphons are proper.

Ant. Eastertide: Alleluia, alleluia, alleluia.
Ant. 1: Love is the fulness of the Law.

PSALM 118(119):97-104 XIII(MEM)

Lórd, how I lóve your láw!*
It is éver in my mínd.
Your commánd makes me wíser than my fóes;*
for it is míne for éver.

I have more ínsight than áll who téach me*
for I pónder your wíll.
I have móre understánding than the óld*
for I kéep your précepts.

I turn my féet from évil páths*
to obéy your wórd.
I háve not túrned from your decrées;*
you yoursélf have táught me.

Your prómise is swéeter to my táste*
than hóney in the móuth.
I gáin understánding from your précepts;*
I háte the ways of fálsehood.

Ant. Love is the fulness of the Law.
Ant. 2: Remember your people, Lord, whom you chose long ago.

LAMENT FOR THE RUINED TEMPLE PSALM 73(74)

Do not be afraid of those who kill the body (Mt 10:28)

I

Whý, O Gód, have you cást us off for éver?*
Whý blaze with ánger at the shéep of your pásture?
Remémber your péople whom you chóse long agó,†
the tríbe you redéemed to be your ówn posséssion,*
the móuntain of Sion where you máde your dwélling.

Turn your stéps to these pláces that are útterly rúined!*
The énemy has laid wáste the whóle of the sánctuary.
Your fóes have made úproar in your hóuse of práyer:†
they have sét up their émblems, their fóreign émblems,*
hígh abóve the éntrance to the sánctuary.

Their áxes have báttered the wóod of its dóors.*
They have strúck togéther with hátchet and píckaxe.
O Gód, they have sét your sánctuary on fíre:*
they have rázed and profáned the pláce where you dwéll.

They sáid in their héarts: 'Let us útterly crúsh them:*
let us búrn every shríne of Gód in the lánd.'
There is no sígn from Gód, nor háve we a próphet,*
we have nó one to téll us how lóng it will lást.

How lóng, O Gód, is the énemy to scóff?*
is the fóe to insúlt your náme for éver?
Whý, O Lórd, do you hóld back your hánd?*
Whý do you kéep your ríght hand hídden?

Yet Gód is our kíng from tíme pást,*
the gíver of hélp through áll the lánd.

Ant. Remember your people, Lord, whom you chose long ago.
Ant. 3: Arise, O Lord, and defend your cause.

II

It was yóu who divíded the séa by your míght,*
who sháttered the héads of the mónsters in the séa.

It was yóu who crúshed Leviathan's héads*
and gáve him as fóod to the úntamed béasts.
It was yóu who ópened spríngs and tórrents;*
it was yóu who dríed up éver-flowing rívers.

Yóurs is the dáy and yóurs is the níght.*
It was yóu who appóinted the líght and the sún:
it was yóu who fíxed the bóunds of the éarth:*
yóu who máde both súmmer and wínter.

Remémber this, Lórd, and see the énemy scóffing;*
a sénseless péople insúlts your náme.
Do not gíve Ísrael, your dóve, to the háwk*
nor forgét the lífe of your póor ones for éver.

Remémber your cóvenant;† every cáve in the lánd*
is a pláce where víolence mákes its hóme.
Do not lét the oppréssed retúrn disappóinted;*
let the póor and the néedy bléss your náme.

Aríse, O Gód, and defénd your cáuse!*
Remémber how the sénseless revíle you all the dáy.
Dó not forgét the clámour of your fóes,*
the dáily incréasing úproar of your fóes.

Ant. Arise, O Lord, and defend your cause.
Eastertide: Alleluia, alleluia, alleluia.

At the other Hours, the complementary psalms from Series I and III.

Through the Year

Before Noon

SCRIPTURE READING JER 22:3

Practise honesty and integrity; rescue the man who has been wronged from the hands of his oppressor; do not exploit the stranger, the orphan, the widow; do no violence; shed no innocent blood.

℣ The Lord will rule the earth with justice.
℟ He will judge the peoples with fairness.

CONCLUDING PRAYER

Almighty, ever-living God,
who at this hour sent down your Holy Spirit on the apostles,
send forth that same Spirit of love into our hearts
so that we may bear faithful witness to you,
before all mankind.
Through Christ our Lord.

Midday

SCRIPTURE READING DEUT 15:7-8

Is there a poor man among you, one of your brothers, in any town of yours? Do not harden your heart or close your hand against that poor brother of yours, but be open-handed with him and lend him enough for his needs.

℣ Lord, you have listened to the prayer of the poor.
℟ You will give ear to them and strengthen their hearts.

CONCLUDING PRAYER

Almighty God,
who revealed to Peter your plan for the salvation of all men,
grant that our work may be acceptable to you,
and that, by your grace, it may further your loving purpose of redemption.
Through Christ our Lord.

Afternoon

SCRIPTURE READING PROV 22:22-23

Do not rob the poor, because he is poor,
or crush the afflicted at the gate;
for the Lord will plead their cause
and despoil of life those who despoil them.

℣ The Lord will save the needy who are helpless.
℟ He will save the lives of the poor.

CONCLUDING PRAYER

Almighty God,
we recall how you sent your angel to the centurion Cornelius
to show him the way of salvation.

Open our hearts to work more zealously
for the salvation of the world,
so that your Church
may bring us and all men into your presence.
Through Christ our Lord.

WEEK 3: WEDNESDAY

Hymn *(see p. 67)*

PSALMODY

In Advent, Christmastide and Lent the antiphons are proper.

Ant. Eastertide: Alleluia, alleluia, alleluia.
Ant. 1: Any man who follows me will not be walking in the dark; he will have the light of life, says the Lord.

PSALM 118(119):105-112 XIV(NUN)

Your wórd is a lámp for my stéps*
and a líght for my páth.
I have swórn and have máde up my mínd*
to obéy your decrées.

Lórd, I am déeply afflícted:*
by your wórd give me lífe.
Accépt, Lord, the hómage of my líps*
and téach me your decrées.

Though I cárry my lífe in my hánds,*
I remémber your láw.
Though the wícked trý to ensnáre me*
I do not stráy from your précepts.

Your wíll is my héritage for éver,*
the jóy of my héart.
I sét myself to cárry out your wíll*
in fúlness, for éver.

Ant. Any man who follows me will not be walking in the dark; he will have the light of life, says the Lord.
Ant. 2: I am wretched and poor; O God, help me.

O GOD, MAKE HASTE TO HELP ME PSALM 69(70)

Lord, save us, for we are in peril (Mt 8:25)

O Gód, make háste to my réscue,*
Lord, cóme to my áid!
Lét there be sháme and confúsion*
on thóse who seek my lífe.

O lét them turn báck in confúsion,*
who delíght in my hárm,
let them retréat, cóvered with sháme,*
who jéer at my lót.

Lét there be rejóicing and gládness*
for áll who séek you.
Let them sáy for ever: 'Gód is gréat,'*
who lóve your saving hélp.

As for mé, wrétched and póor,*
cóme to me, O Gód.
Yóu are my réscuer, my hélp,*
O Lórd, do not deláy.

Ant. I am wretched and poor; O God, help me.
Ant. 3: God will not judge by appearances, but he will rule with justice and fairness.

THE LORD IS RULER OF ALL PSALM 74(75)

He put down princes from their thrones and exalted the lowly (Lk 1:52)

We give thánks to yóu, O Gód,†
we give thánks and cáll upon your náme.*
We recóunt your wónderful déeds.

'When I réach the appóinted tíme,*
thén I will júdge with jústice.

Though the éarth and all who dwéll in it may róck,*
it is Í who uphóld its píllars.

To the bóastful I say: "Do not bóast,"*
to the wícked: "Do not fláunt your stréngth,
do not fláunt your stréngth on hígh.*
Do not spéak with ínsolent príde."'

For néither from the éast nor from the wést,*
nor from désert or móuntains comes júdgment,
but Gód himsélf is the júdge.*
One he húmbles, anóther he exálts.

The Lórd holds a cúp in his hánd,*
full of wíne, fóaming and spíced.
He póurs it; they drínk it to the drégs:*
all the wícked on the éarth must dráin it.

As for mé, I will rejóice for éver*
and sing psálms to Jácob's Gód.
He shall bréak the pówer of the wícked,*
while the stréngth of the júst shall be exálted.

Ant. God will not judge by appearances, but he will rule with justice and fairness.
Eastertide: Alleluia, alleluia, alleluia.

At the other Hours, the complementary psalms.

Through the Year

Before Noon

SCRIPTURE READING 1 COR 13:4-7

Love is always patient and kind; it is never jealous; love is never boastful or conceited; it is never rude or selfish; it does not take offence, and is not resentful. Love takes no pleasure in other people's sins but delights in the truth; it is always ready to excuse, to trust, to hope, and to endure whatever comes.

℣ Let there be rejoicing and gladness for all who seek you, Lord.
℟ Let them say for ever: 'God is great.'

CONCLUDING PRAYER

Lord, holy Father, faithful to your promise
you sent your Spirit
to bring together a people divided by sin.
Give us grace to foster unity and peace among men.
Through Christ our Lord.

Midday

SCRIPTURE READING 1 COR 13:8-9,13

Love does not come to an end. But if there are gifts of prophecy, the time will come when they must fail. For our knowledge is imperfect and our prophesying is imperfect; but once perfection comes, all imperfect things will disappear. Meanwhile there are three things that last: faith, hope and love; and the greatest of these is love.

℣ May your love be upon us, O Lord.
℟ We place all our hope in you.

CONCLUDING PRAYER

God of power and love,
look kindly on the tasks we have begun,
and at this midday hour renew your grace within us:
make good our defects
and bring our work to that fulfilment
which accords with your will.
Through Christ our Lord.

Afternoon

SCRIPTURE READING COL 3:14-15

And to all these add love, which binds all things together in perfect unity. The peace that Christ gives is to be the judge in your hearts; for to this peace God has called you together in the one body. And be thankful.

℣ The humble shall inherit the land.
℟ They shall enjoy the fulness of peace.

CONCLUDING PRAYER

On the cross, Lord Jesus Christ,
you stretched out your hands for the salvation of the human race;

grant that our life and work
may be pleasing to you
and bear witness to the power of your redeeming love.
Who live and reign for ever and ever.

WEEK 3: THURSDAY

Hymn *(see p. 67)*

PSALMODY

In Advent, Christmastide and Lent the antiphons are proper.

Ant. Eastertide: Alleluia, alleluia, alleluia.
Ant. 1: Uphold me by your promise, Lord, and I shall live.

PSALM 118(119):113-120 XV (SAMECH)

I have no lóve for hálf-hearted mén:*
my lóve is for your láw.
Yóu are my shélter, my shíeld;*
I hópe in your wórd.

Léave me, yóu who do évil;*
I will kéep God's commánd.
If you uphóld me by your prómise I shall líve;*
let my hópes not be in váin.

Sustáin me and Í shall be sáved*
and ever obsérve your commánds.
You spúrn all who swérve from your státutes;*
their cúnning is in váin.

You thrów away the wícked like dróss:*
so I lóve your wíll.
I trémble befóre you in térror;*
I féar your decrées.

Ant. Uphold me by your promise, Lord, and I shall live.
Ant. 2: Come to our help, O God our saviour, and forgive us our sins.

LAMENT FOR JERUSALEM — PSALM 78(79):1-5,8-11,13

If you had only understood the message of peace (Lk 19:42)

O Gód, the nátions have inváded your lánd,†
they háve profáned your hóly témple.*
They have máde Jerúsalem a héap of rúins.
They have hánded óver the bódies of your sérvants†
as fóod to féed the bírds of héaven*
and the flésh of your fáithful to the béasts of the éarth.

They have póured out blóod like wáter in Jerúsalem,*
nó one is léft to búry the déad.
Wé have becóme the táunt of our néighbours,*
the móckery and scórn of thóse who surróund us.
How lóng, O Lórd? Will you be ángry for éver,*
how lóng will your ánger búrn like fíre?

Do not hóld the guílt of our fáthers agáinst us.†
Lét your compássion hásten to méet us*
wé are léft in the dépths of distréss.
O Gód our sáviour, cóme to our hélp,*
cóme for the sáke of the glóry of your náme.
O Lórd our Gód, forgíve us our síns;*
réscue ús for the sáke of your náme.

Whý should the nátions say:* 'Whére is their Gód?'
Let us sée the nátions aróund us repáid*
with véngeance for the blóod of your sérvants that was shéd!
Let the gróans of the prísoners cóme befóre you;*
let your stróng arm repríeve those condémned to díe.

But wé, your péople, the flóck of your pásture,†
will gíve you thánks for éver and éver.*
We will téll your práise from áge to áge.

Ant. Come to our help, O God our saviour, and forgive us our sins.
Ant. 3: God of hosts, look down from heaven, and come to visit this vine of yours.

LORD, COME TO VISIT YOUR VINE
PSALM 79(80)

Come, Lord Jesus (Rev 22:20)

O shépherd of Ísrael, héar us,*
you who léad Jóseph's flóck,
shine fórth from your chérubim thróne*
upon Éphraim, Bénjamin, Manásseh.
O Lórd, róuse up your míght,*
O Lórd, cóme to our hélp.

Gód of hósts, bríng us báck;*
let your fáce shine on ús and wé shall be sáved.

Lórd God of hósts, how lóng*
will you frówn on your péople's pléa?
You have féd them with téars for their bréad,*
an abúndance of téars for their drínk.
You have máde us the táunt of our néighbours,*
our énemies láugh us to scórn.

Gód of hósts, bríng us báck;*
let your fáce shine on ús and wé shall be sáved.

You bróught a víne out of Égypt;*
to plánt it you dróve out the nátions.
Befóre it you cléared the gróund;*
it took róot and spréad through the lánd.

The móuntains were cóvered with its shádow,*
the cédars of Gód with its bóughs.
It strétched out its bránches to the séa,*
to the Great Ríver it strétched out its shóots.

Then whý have you bróken down its wálls?*
It is plúcked by áll who pass bý.
It is rávaged by the bóar of the fórest,*
devóured by the béasts of the fíeld.

God of hósts, turn agáin, we implóre,*
look dówn from héaven and sée.

Vísit this víne and protéct it,*
the víne your ríght hand has plánted.
Men have búrnt it with fíre and destróyed it.*
May they pérish at the frówn of your fáce.

May your hánd be on the mán you have chósen,*
the mán you have gíven your stréngth.
And we shall néver forsáke you agáin:*
give us lífe that we may cáll upon your náme.

Gód of hósts, bríng us báck;*
let your fáce shine on ús and wé shall be sáved.

Ant. God of hosts, look down from heaven, and come to visit this vine of yours.
Eastertide: Alleluia, alleluia, alleluia.

At the other Hours, the complementary psalms.

Through the Year

Before Noon

SCRIPTURE READING WIS 19:20b

Yes, Lord, in every way you have made your people great and glorious; you have never disdained them, but stood by them always and everywhere.

℣ You are the God who works wonders.
℟ You have made known to the peoples your might.

CONCLUDING PRAYER

Lord, who at this hour
bestowed the gift of the Holy Spirit on the apostles while they were at prayer:
grant us a share in that same grace.
Through Christ our Lord.

Midday

SCRIPTURE READING DEUT 4:7

What great nation is there that has its gods so near as the Lord our God is to us whenever we call to him?

℣ The Lord is close to those who call upon him.
℟ He will listen to their prayer.

CONCLUDING PRAYER
Almighty God,
you are all light,
in you there is no darkness.
Let your light shine upon us in all its radiance,
so that we may walk gladly in the way of your commandments.
Through Christ our Lord.

Afternoon

SCRIPTURE READING ESTHER 10:9

The single nation, mine, is Israel, those who cried out to God and were saved. Yes, the Lord has saved his people, the Lord has delivered us from all these evils, God has worked such signs and great wonders as have never happened among the nations.

℣ I will praise you, Lord, you have listened to my prayer.
℟ You have become my saviour.

CONCLUDING PRAYER
Lord, in answer to our prayer
give us patience in suffering hardships
after the example of your Only-begotten Son,
who lives and reigns for ever and ever.

WEEK 3: FRIDAY

Hymn *(see p. 67)*

PSALMODY

In Advent, Christmastide and Lent the antiphons are proper.

Ant. Eastertide: Alleluia, alleluia, alleluia.
Ant. 1: We saw him despised by men, a man of sorrows and acquainted with grief.

WHEN THE JUST MAN CALLS, THE LORD LISTENS PSALM 21(22)

Jesus cried out in a loud voice, 'Eli, Eli, lama sabachthani?' (Mt 27:46)

I

My Gód, my Gód, whý have you forsáken me?*
You are fár from my pléa and the crý of my distréss.
O my Gód, I call by dáy and you gíve no replý;*
I cáll by níght and I fínd no péace.

Yet yóu, O Gód, are hóly,*
enthróned on the práises of Ísrael.
In yóu our fáthers put their trúst;*
they trústed and you sét them frée.
When they críed to yóu, they escáped.*
In you they trústed and néver in váin.

But Í am a wórm and no mán,*
scorned by mén, despísed by the péople.
Áll who sée me deríde me.*
They curl their líps, they tóss their héads.
'He trústed in the Lórd, let him sáve him;*
let him reléase him if thís is his fríend.'

Yes, it was yóu who tóok me from the wómb,*
entrústed me to my móther's bréast.
To yóu I was commítted from my bírth,*
from my móther's womb yóu have been my Gód.
Do not léave me alóne in my distréss;*
come clóse, there is nóne else to hélp.

Ant. We saw him despised by men, a man of sorrows and acquainted with grief.
Ant. 2: They shared his clothes among them by casting lots.

II

Mány búlls have surróunded me,*
fierce búlls of Báshan close me ín.
Agáinst me they ópen wide their jáws,*
like líons, rénding and róaring.

Like wáter Í am poured óut,*
disjóinted are áll my bónes.
My héart has becóme like wáx,*
it is mélted withín my bréast.

Párched as burnt cláy is my thróat,*
my tóngue cléaves to my jáws.
Mány dógs have surróunded me,*
a bánd of the wícked besét me.
They tear hóles in my hánds and my féet*
and láy me in the dúst of déath.

I can cóunt every óne of my bónes.*
These péople stáre at me and glóat;
they divíde my clóthing amóng them.*
They cást lóts for my róbe.

O Lórd, do not léave me alóne,*
my stréngth, make háste to hélp me!
Réscue my sóul from the swórd,*
my lífe from the gríp of these dógs.
Save my lífe from the jáws of these líons,*
my poor sóul from the hórns of these óxen.

I will téll of your náme to my bréthren*
and práise you where théy are assémbled.

Ant. They shared his clothes among them by casting lots.
Ant. 3: All families of the nations will worship before the Lord.

III

'You who féar the Lórd give him práise;†
all sóns of Jácob, give him glóry.*
Revére him, Ísrael's sóns.

For hé has néver despísed*
nor scórned the póverty of the póor.
From hím he has not hídden his fáce,*
but he héard the póor man when he críed.'

Yóu are my práise in the gréat assémbly.*
My vóws I will páy before thóse who féar him.

The póor shall éat and shall háve their fíll.†
They shall práise the Lórd, thóse who séek him.*
May their héarts líve for éver and éver!

All the éarth shall remémber and retúrn to the Lórd,†
all fámilies of the nátions wórship befóre him*
for the kíngdom is the Lórd's; he is rúler of the nátions.
They shall wórship him, áll the míghty of the éarth;*
befóre him shall bów all who go dówn to the dúst.

And my sóul shall live for hím,* my chíldren sérve him.
They shall téll of the Lórd to generátions yet to cóme,†
decláre his fáithfulness to péoples yet unbórn:*
'Thése things the Lórd has dóne.'

Ant. All families of the nations will worship before the Lord.
Eastertide: Alleluia, alleluia, alleluia.

At the other Hours, the complementary psalms.

Through the Year

Before Noon

SCRIPTURE READING ROM 1:16b-17

The Good News is the power of God saving all who have faith, since this is what reveals the justice of God to us: it shows how faith leads to faith, or as scripture says: The upright man finds life through faith.

℣ In the Lord our hearts will find joy.
℟ We have put our trust in his holy name.

CONCLUDING PRAYER

Lord Jesus Christ,
at this hour you were led to the cross
to suffer the penalty of death
for the salvation of mankind:
in your mercy grant us pardon for our past offences
and by your power preserve us from future falls.
Who live and reign for ever and ever.

Midday

SCRIPTURE READING ROM 3:21-22a

God's justice that was made known through the Law and the Prophets has now been revealed outside the Law, since it is the same justice of God that comes through faith to everyone who believes in Jesus Christ.

℣ The precepts of the Lord are right, they gladden the heart.
℟ The command of the Lord is clear, it gives light to the eye.

CONCLUDING PRAYER

Lord Jesus Christ,
who at this hour
when the whole world was shrouded in darkness
mounted the wood of the cross
as the innocent victim for our redemption,
give us always that light
which will bring us to eternal life.
Who live and reign for ever and ever.

Afternoon

SCRIPTURE READING EPH 2:8-9

It is by God's grace that you have been saved, through faith. It is not your own doing, but God's gift. There is nothing here to boast of, since it is not the result of your own efforts.

℣ Lord, let your way be known on earth.
℟ Let all nations know your salvation.

CONCLUDING PRAYER

Lord Jesus Christ,
who on the cross called the penitent thief into your kingdom,
in faith and trust and confessing our sins
we implore your mercy
that after our death
you will lead us rejoicing through the gates of paradise.
Who live and reign for ever and ever.

WEEK 3: SATURDAY

Hymn *(see p. 67)*

PSALMODY

In Advent, Christmastide and Lent the antiphons are proper.

Ant. Eastertide: Alleluia, alleluia, alleluia.
Ant. 1: Lord, vouch for the welfare of your servant.

PSALM 118(119):121-128 XVI (AIN)

I have dóne what is ríght and júst:*
let me nót be oppréssed.
Vóuch for the wélfare of your sérvant*
lest the próud oppréss me.

My eyes yéarn for your sáving hélp*
and the prómise of your jústice.
Tréat your sérvant with lóve*
and téach me your commánds.

Í am your sérvant, give me knówledge;*
then I shall knów your wíll.
It is tíme for the Lórd to áct*
for your láw has been bróken.

Thát is why I lóve your commánds*
more than fínest góld,
why I rúle my lífe by your précepts:*
I háte the ways of fálsehood.

Ant. Lord, vouch for the welfare of your servant.
Ant. 2: Look to the Lord and be radiant.

THE LORD IS THE SALVATION OF THE JUST PSALM 33(34)

You have tasted and seen that the Lord is sweet (1 Pet 2:3)

I

I will bléss the Lórd at all tímes,*

his práise álways on my líps;
in the Lórd my sóul shall make its bóast.*
The húmble shall héar and be glád.

Glórify the Lórd with mé.*
Togéther let us práise his náme.
I sóught the Lórd and he ánswered me;*
from all my térrors he sét me frée.

Lóok towards hím and be rádiant;*
let your fáces nót be abáshed.
This póor man cálled; the Lord héard him*
and réscued him from áll his distréss.

The ángel of the Lórd is encámped*
around thóse who revére him, to réscue them.
Taste and sée that the Lórd is góod.*
He is háppy who seeks réfuge in hím.

Revére the Lórd, you his sáints.*
They lack nóthing, thóse who revére him.
Strong líons suffer wánt and go húngry*
but thóse who seek the Lórd lack no bléssing.

Ant. Look to the Lord and be radiant.
Ant. 3: The Lord is close to the broken-hearted.

II

Cóme, chíldren, and héar me*
that I may téach you the féar of the Lórd.
Who is hé who lóngs for lífe*
and many dáys, to enjóy his prospérity?

Then kéep your tóngue from évil*
and your líps from spéaking decéit.
Turn asíde from évil and do góod;*
séek and stríve after péace.

The Lórd turns his fáce against the wícked*
to destróy their remémbrance from the éarth.
The Lórd turns his éyes to the júst*
and his éars to théir appéal.

They cáll and the Lórd héars*
and réscues them in áll their distréss.
The Lord is clóse to the bróken-héarted;*
those whose spírit is crúshed he will sáve.

Mány are the tríals of the júst man*
but from them áll the Lórd will réscue him.
He will keep guárd over áll his bónes,*
not óne of his bónes shall be bróken.

Évil brings déath to the wícked;*
those who háte the góod are dóomed.
The Lord ránsoms the sóuls of his sérvants.*
Those who híde in him shall nót be condémned.

Ant. The Lord is close to the broken-hearted.
Ant. Eastertide: Alleluia, alleluia, alleluia.

At the other Hours, the complementary psalms from Series II and III.

Through the Year

Before Noon

SCRIPTURE READING 1 SAM 15:22

Can the Lord's favour be won by offering him sacrifice and victim, instead of obeying his divine will? The Lord loves obedience better than any sacrifice, the attentive ear better than the fat of rams.

℣ A sacrifice of praise will give me honour.
℟ I will show God's salvation to the upright.

CONCLUDING PRAYER

Send forth the light of the Holy Spirit on us,
Lord God, almighty Father,
subject as we are to your divine majesty:
so that safe from every foe,
we may always rejoice
as we celebrate your praise.
Through Christ our Lord.

Midday

SCRIPTURE READING GAL 5:26;6:2

We must not indulge vain ambitions, envying one another and provoking one another to envy. Bear the burden of one another's failings; then you will be fulfilling the law of Christ.

℣ How good and how pleasant it is, brothers dwelling in unity.
℟ There the Lord gives his blessing.

CONCLUDING PRAYER

Lord God,
living light of eternal love,
grant that always aglow with charity,
we may love you above all else
and our brethren for your sake,
with one and the selfsame love.
Through Christ our Lord.

Afternoon

SCRIPTURE READING MIC 6:8

What is good I will make known to you, man;
this is what the Lord asks of you:
only this, to act justly,
to love tenderly
and to walk humbly with your God.
℣ I take delight in your ways, Lord.
℟ I will not forget your word.

CONCLUDING PRAYER

Give us perfect peace, Lord,
so that we may delight in serving you
all the days of our life,
and at the last, with our Lady's help,
come safely to your presence.
Through Christ our Lord.

WEEK 4: SUNDAY

HYMN

Eternal Father, loving God,
Who made us from the dust of earth,
Transform us by the Spirit's grace,
Give value to our little worth.

Prepare us for that day of days
When Christ from heaven will come with might
To call us out of dust again,
Our bodies glorified in light.

O Godhead, here untouched, unseen,
All things created bear your trace;
The seed of glory sown in man
Will flower when we see your face.

PSALMODY

In Advent, Christmastide and Lent the antiphons are proper.

Ant. Eastertide: Alleluia, alleluia, alleluia.
Ant. 1: Whoever eats this bread will live for ever, alleluia.

THE GOOD SHEPHERD — PSALM 22(23)

The Lamb is their king who leads them to the source of the water of life (Rev 7:17)

The Lórd is my shépherd;*
there is nóthing I shall wánt.
Frésh and gréen are the pástures*
where he gíves me repóse.
Near réstful wáters he léads me,*
To revíve my drooping spírit.

He guídes me alóng the right páth;*
he is trúe to his náme.
If I should wálk in the válley of dárkness*
no évil would I féar.

You are thére with your cróok and your stáff;*
with thése you give me cómfort.

You have prepáred a bánquet for mé*
in the síght of my fóes.
My héad you have anóinted with óil;*
my cúp is overflówing.

Surely góodness and kíndness shall fóllow me*
all the dáys of my lífe.
In the Lórd's own hóuse shall I dwéll*
for éver and éver.

Ant. Whoever eats this bread will live for ever, alleluia.
Ant. 2: The Lord will come in glory and he will do wonderful things for his saints, alleluia.

THANKSGIVING FOR VICTORY PSALM 75(76)

They will see the Son of Man coming on the clouds of heaven (Mt 24:30)

I

Gód is made knówn in Júdah;*
in Ísrael his náme is gréat.
He sét up his tént in Jerúsalem*
and his dwélling pláce in Síon.
It was thére he bróke the flashing árrows,*
the shíeld, the swórd, the ármour.

Yóu, O Lórd, are resplêndent,*
more majéstic than the éverlasting móuntains.
The wárriors, despóiled, slept in déath;*
the hánds of the sóldiers were pówerless.
At your thréat, O Gód of Jácob,*
hórse and ríder lay stúnned.

Ant. The Lord will come in glory and he will do wonderful things for his saints, alleluia.
Ant. 3: Offer prayers and gifts to the Lord your God, alleluia.

II

Yóu, you alóne, strike térror.*
Who shall stánd when your ánger is róused?
You úttered your séntence from the héavens;*
the éarth in térror was stíll
when Gód aróse to júdge,*
to sáve the húmble of the éarth.

Men's ánger will sérve to práise you;†
its survívors surróund you in jóy.*
Make vóws to your Gód and fulfíl them.
Let all pay tríbute to hím who strikes térror,†
who cúts short the lífe of prínces,*
who strikes térror in the kíngs of the éarth.

Ant. Offer prayers and gifts to the Lord your God, alleluia.
Eastertide: Alleluia, alleluia, alleluia.

At the other Hours, the complementary psalms.

Through the Year

Before Noon

SCRIPTURE READING 1 COR 6:19-20

Your body, you know, is the temple of the Holy Spirit, who is in you since you received him from God. You are not your own property; you have been bought and paid for. That is why you should use your body for the glory of God.

℣ My soul is longing and yearning for the courts of the Lord.
℟ My heart and my soul ring out their joy to the living God.

Midday

SCRIPTURE READING DEUT 10:12

What does the Lord your God ask of you? Only this: to fear the Lord your God, to follow all his ways, to love him, to serve the Lord your God with all your heart and all your soul.

℣ Lord, who shall be admitted to your holy place?
℟ He who walks without fault and speaks the truth from his heart.

Afternoon

SCRIPTURE READING SONG 8:6b-7

Love is strong as death,
passion cruel as the grave;
it blazes up like a blazing fire,
fiercer than any flame.
Many waters cannot quench love,
no flood can sweep it away.
℣ I love you, Lord, my strength.
℟ You are my protector and my mighty saviour.

The concluding prayer from the Proper of Seasons.

WEEK 4: MONDAY

Hymn *(see p. 96)*

PSALMODY

In Advent, Christmastide and Lent the antiphons are proper.

Ant. Eastertide: Alleluia, alleluia, alleluia.
Ant. 1: Let my steps be guided by your promise, O Lord.

MEDITATION ON THE WORD OF GOD IN THE LAW PSALM 118(119):129-136 XVII (PE)

Love is the Law in all its fulness (Rom 13:10)

Your wíll is wónderful indéed;*
thérefore I obéy it.
The unfólding of your wórd gives líght*
and téaches the símple.

I ópen my móuth and I sígh*
as I yéarn for your commánds.
Túrn and shów me your mércy;*
show jústice to your fríends.

Let my stéps be guíded by your prómise;*
let no évil rúle me.

Redéem me from mán's oppréssion*
and Í will keep your précepts.

Let your fáce shíne on your sérvant*
and téach me your decrées.
Téars stréam from my éyes*
because your láw is disobéyed.

Ant. Let my steps be guided by your promise, O Lord.
Ant. 2: There is but one judge and one ruler: who, then, are you to judge your neighbour?

AGAINST CORRUPT AUTHORITY — PSALM 81(82)

Let there be no premature passing of judgment; leave that until the Lord comes (1 Cor 4:5)

God stánds in the divíne assémbly.*
In the mídst of the góds he gives júdgment.

'How lóng will you júdge unjústly*
and fávour the cáuse of the wícked?
Do jústice for the wéak and the órphan,*
defénd the afflícted and the néedy.
Réscue the wéak and the póor;*
set them frée from the hánd of the wícked.

Unpercéiving, they grópe in the dárkness*
and the órder of the wórld is sháken.
I have sáid to you: "Yóu are góds*
and áll of you, sóns of the Most Hígh."
And yét, you shall díe like mén,*
you shall fáll like ány of the prínces.'

Aríse, O Gód, judge the éarth,*
for yóu rule áll the nátions.

Ant. There is but one judge and one ruler: who, then, are you to judge your neighbour?
Ant. 3: I called, and the Lord heard me.

LONGING FOR PEACE PSALM 119(120)

Show patience in times of trouble; never cease praying (Rom 12:12)

To the Lórd in the hóur of my distréss*
I cáll and he ánswers me.
'O Lórd, save my sóul from lying líps,*
from the tóngue of the decéitful.'

Whát shall he páy you in retúrn,*
O tréacherous tóngue?
The wárrior's árrows shárpened*
and cóals, red-hot, blázing.

Alas, that I abíde a stránger in Méshech,*
dwell among the ténts of Kédar!

Long enóugh have Í been dwélling*
with thóse who hate péace.
Í am for péace, but when I spéak,*
théy are for fíghting.

Ant. I called, and the Lord heard me.
Eastertide: Alleluia, alleluia, alleluia.

At the other Hours, the complementary psalms from Series II and III.

Through the Year

Before Noon

SCRIPTURE READING LEV 20:26

You shall be holy to me; for I the Lord am holy, and have separated you from the peoples, that you should be mine.

℣ Blessed is the people whose God is the Lord.
℟ The people he has chosen for his own.

CONCLUDING PRAYER

Father, Creator of all that is good,
you have called men to work in your world,
and by their co-operation to better the condition of mankind.
Grant that we may always work together as children of your family,

and love all men as our brethren.
Through Christ our Lord.

Midday

SCRIPTURE READING WIS 15:1,3

You, our God, are kind, loyal and slow to anger,
and you govern all things with mercy.
To acknowledge you is indeed the perfect virtue,
to know your power is the root of immortality.
℣ You, Lord, are a God of love and mercy.
℟ You are patient, full of loving kindness and truth.

CONCLUDING PRAYER

God, Lord and master of the vineyard,
you allot us our tasks
and determine the just rewards of our labours.
Help us to bear the burden of the day
and accept your will in all things without complaint.
Through Christ our Lord.

Afternoon

SCRIPTURE READING BAR 4:21-22

Take courage, my children, call on God:
he will deliver you from tyranny,
from the hands of your enemies;
for I look to the Eternal for your rescue,
and joy has come to me from the Holy One
at the mercy soon to reach you
from your saviour, the Eternal.
℣ Remember your mercy, Lord.
℟ Do not forget the love you have shown from of old.

CONCLUDING PRAYER

God our Father,
you are calling us to prayer,
at that same hour
when the apostles went up to the temple.
Grant that the prayer we offer with sincere hearts

in the name of Jesus,
may bring salvation to all who call upon that holy Name.
Through Christ our Lord.

WEEK 4: TUESDAY

Hymn *(see p. 96)*

PSALMODY

In Advent, Christmastide and Lent the antiphons are proper.

Ant. Eastertide: Alleluia, alleluia, alleluia.
Ant. 1: Since you know the will of God, act according to it and you will be blessed.

PSALM 118(119):137-144 XVIII(SADE)

Lórd, you are júst indéed;*
your decrées are ríght.
You have impósed your wíll with jústice*
and with ábsolute trúth.

I am cárried awáy by ánger*
for my fóes forget your wórd.
Your prómise is tríed in the fíre,*
the delíght of your sérvant.

Althóugh I am wéak and despísed*
I remémber your précepts.
Your jústice is etérnal jústice*
and your láw is trúth.

Though ánguish and distréss have séized me,*
I delíght in your commánds.
The jústice of your wíll is etérnal:*
if you téach me, I shall líve.

Ant. Since you know the will of God, act according to it and you will be blessed.
Ant. 2: Let my prayer come into your presence, O Lord.

PRAYER OF ONE WHO IS GRAVELY ILL PSALM 87(88)

This is your hour; this is the reign of darkness (Lk 22:53)

I

Lord my Gód, I call for hélp by dáy;*
I crý at níght befóre you.
Let my práyer cóme into your présence.*
O túrn your éar to my crý.

For my sóul is fílled with évils;*
my lífe is on the brínk of the gráve.
I am réckoned as óne in the tómb:*
I have réached the énd of my stréngth,

like óne alóne among the déad;*
like the sláin lýing in their gráves;
like thóse you remémber no móre,*
cut óff, as they áre, from your hánd.

You have láid me in the dépths of the tómb,*
in pláces that are dárk, in the dépths.
Your ánger weighs dówn upón me:*
I am drówned benéath your wáves.

Ant. Let my prayer come into your presence, O Lord.
Ant. 3: To you, O Lord, I call for help: do not hide your face from me.

II

You have táken awáy my fríends*
and máde me hátefl in their síght.
Imprísoned, I cánnot escápe;*
my éyes are súnken with gríef.

I cáll to you, Lórd, all the day lóng;*
to yóu I strétch out my hánds.
Will you wórk your wónders for the déad?*
Will the shádes stánd and práise you?

Will your lóve be tóld in the gráve*
or your fáithfulness amóng the déad?
Will your wónders be knówn in the dárk*

or your jústice in the lánd of oblívion?

As for mé, Lord, I cáll to you for hélp:*
in the mórning my práyer comes befóre you.
Lórd, whý do you rejéct me?*
Whý do you híde your fáce?

Wrétched, close to déath from my yóuth,*
I have bórne your tríals; I am númb.
Your fúry has swépt down upón me;*
your térrors have útterly destróyed me.

They surróund me all the dáy like a flóod,*
they assáil me áll togéther.
Friend and néighbour you have táken awáy:*
my óne compánion is dárkness.

Ant. To you, O Lord, I call for help: do not hide your face from me.
Eastertide: Alleluia, alleluia, alleluia.

At the other Hours, the complementary psalms.

Through the Year

Before Noon

SCRIPTURE READING 1 JN 3:17-18

If a man who was rich enough in this world's goods
saw that one of his brothers was in need,
but closed his heart to him,
how could the love of God be living in him?
My children,
our love is not to be just words or mere talk,
but something real and active.
℣ Happy is the man who shows mercy and compassion.
℟ He will be remembered for ever.

CONCLUDING PRAYER

Almighty, ever-living God,
who at this hour sent down your Holy Spirit on the apostles,
send forth that same Spirit of love into our hearts

so that we may bear faithful witness to you,
before all mankind.
Through Christ our Lord.

Midday

SCRIPTURE READING DEUT 30:11,14

This Law that I enjoin on you today is not beyond your strength or beyond your reach. No, the Word is very near to you, it is in your mouth and in your heart for your observance.

℣ Your word, Lord, gives light for my feet.
℟ It shows me the way I should walk.

CONCLUDING PRAYER

Almighty God,
who revealed to Peter your plan for the salvation of all men,
grant that our work may be acceptable to you,
and that, by your grace, it may further your loving purpose of redemption.
Through Christ our Lord.

Afternoon

SCRIPTURE READING IS 55:10-11

As the rain and the snow come down from the heavens and do not return without watering the earth, making it yield and giving growth to provide seed for the sower and bread for the eating, so the word that goes from my mouth does not return to me empty, without carrying out my will and succeeding in what it was sent to do.

℣ The Lord has sent out his word to the earth.
℟ His command runs swiftly.

CONCLUDING PRAYER

Almighty God,
we recall how you sent your angel to the centurion Cornelius
to show him the way of salvation.
Open our hearts to work more zealously
for the salvation of the world,
so that your Church
may bring us and all men into your presence.
Through Christ our Lord.

WEEK 4: WEDNESDAY

Hymn *(see p. 96)*

PSALMODY

In Advent, Christmastide and Lent the antiphons are proper.

Ant. Eastertide: Alleluia, alleluia, alleluia.
Ant. 1: I called to you, O Lord; in your word I put my trust.

PSALM 118(119):145-152 XIX (KOPH)

I cáll with all my héart; Lord, héar me,*
I will kéep your commánds.
I cáll upón you, sáve me*
and Í will do your wíll.

I ríse before dáwn and cry for hélp,*
I hópe in your wórd.
My éyes wátch through the níght*
to pónder your prómise.

In your lóve hear my vóice, O Lórd;*
give me lífe by your decrées.
Those who hárm me unjústly draw néar:*
they are fár from your láw.

But yóu, O Lórd, are clóse:*
your commánds are trúth.
Lóng have I knówn that your wíll*
is estáblished for éver.

Ant. I called to you, O Lord; in your word I put my trust.
Ant. 2: The Lord knows the thoughts of men. He knows they are no more than a breath.

THE LORD IS THE VINDICATOR OF THE JUST PSALM 93(94)

The Lord always punishes sins: for God has called us to be holy, not to be immoral (1 Thess 4:6-7)

I

O Lórd, avénging Gód,*
avénging Gód, appéar!
Júdge of the éarth, arise,*
gíve the próud what they desérve!

How lóng, O Lórd, shall the wícked,*
how lóng shall the wícked tríumph?
They blúster with árrogant spéech;*
the évil-doers bóast to each óther.

They crúsh your péople, Lórd,*
they afflíct the ónes you have chósen.
They kíll the wídow and the stránger*
and múrder the fátherless chíld.

And they sáy: 'The Lórd does not sée;*
the God of Jácob páys no héed.'
Mark thís, most sénseless of péople;*
fóols, when wíll you understánd?

Can hé who made the éar, not héar?*
Can hé who formed the éye, not sée?
Will hé who corrects nátions, not púnish?*
Will hé who teaches mén, not have knówledge?
The Lórd knows the thóughts of mén.*
He knóws they are no móre than a bréath.

Ant. The Lord knows the thoughts of men. He knows they are no more than a breath.
Ant. 3: The Lord has become a stronghold for me, a mighty help in whom I place my trust.

II

Happy the mán whom you téach, O Lórd,*
whom you tráin by méans of your láw:
to hím you give péace in evil dáys*
while the pít is being dúg for the wícked.

The Lórd will not abándon his péople*
nor forsáke thóse who are his ówn:
for júdgment shall agáin be júst*
and áll true héarts shall uphóld it.

Who will stánd up for mé against the wícked?*
Who will defénd me from thóse who do évil?
If the Lórd were nót to hélp me,*
I would sóon go dówn into the sílence.

When I thínk: 'I have lóst my fóothold';*
your mércy, Lórd, holds me úp.
When cáres incréase in my héart*
your consolátion cálms my sóul.

Can júdges who do évil be your fríends?*
They do injústice under cóver of láw;
they attáck the lífe of the júst*
and condémn ínnocent blóod.

As for mé, the Lórd will be a strónghold;*
my Gód will be the róck where I take réfuge.
He will repáy them fór their wíckedness,†
destróy them for their évil déeds.*
The Lórd, our Gód, will destróy them.

Ant. The Lord has become a stronghold for me, a mighty help in whom I place my trust.
Eastertide: Alleluia, alleluia, alleluia.

At the other Hours, the complementary psalms.

Through the Year

Before Noon

SCRIPTURE READING 1 COR 10:24,31

Nobody should be looking for his own advantage, but everybody for the other man's. Whatever you eat, whatever you drink, whatever you do at all, do it for the glory of God.

℣ It is good to give praise to the Lord.
℟ To make music to your name, O Most High.

CONCLUDING PRAYER

Lord, holy Father, faithful to your promise
you sent your Spirit
to bring together a people divided by sin.
Give us grace to foster unity and peace among men.
Through Christ our Lord.

Midday

SCRIPTURE READING COL 3:17

Everything you do or say should be done in the name of the Lord Jesus, as you give thanks through him to God the Father.

℣ To you, Lord, I will offer a sacrifice of praise.
℟ I will call upon your name.

CONCLUDING PRAYER

God of power and love,
look kindly on the tasks we have begun,
and at this midday hour renew your grace within us:
make good our defects
and bring our work to that fulfilment
which accords with your will.
Through Christ our Lord.

Afternoon

SCRIPTURE READING COL 3:23-24

Whatever you do, work at it with all your heart, as though you were working for the Lord, and not for men. Remember that the Lord will reward you; you will receive what he has kept for his people. For Christ

is the real Master you serve.
℣ The Lord is my portion and cup.
℟ It is you who mark out my lot.

CONCLUDING PRAYER
On the cross, Lord Jesus Christ,
you stretched out your hands for the salvation of the human race;
grant that our life and work
may be pleasing to you
and bear witness to the power of your redeeming love.
Who live and reign for ever and ever.

WEEK 4: THURSDAY

Hymn *(see p. 96)*

PSALMODY

In Advent, Christmastide and Lent the antiphons are proper.

Ant. Eastertide: Alleluia, alleluia, alleluia.
Ant. 1: If you love me, keep my commandments, says the Lord.

PSALM 118(119):153-160 XX(RESH)

Sée my afflíction and sáve me*
for I remémber your láw.
Uphóld my cáuse and defénd me;*
by your prómise give me lífe.

Salvátion is fár from the wicked*
who are héedless of your commánds.
Númberless, Lórd, are your mércies;*
with your decrées give me lífe.

Though my fóes and oppréssors are cóuntless*
I have not swérved from your wíll.
I lóok at the fáithless with disgúst;*
they ignóre your prómise.

Sée how I lóve your précepts;*
in your mércy give me lífe.
Your wórd is fóunded on trúth:*
your decrées are etérnal.

Ant. If you love me, keep my commandments, says the Lord.
Ant. 2: May the Lord bless you and may you see peace all the days of your life.

PEACE IN THE HOME, A GIFT FROM THE LORD PSALM 127(128)

'May the Lord bless you from Sion', that is, from his Church (Arnobius)

O bléssed are thóse who fear the Lórd*
and wálk in his wáys!

By the lábour of your hánds you shall éat.*
You will be háppy and prósper;
your wífe like a frúitful víne*
in the héart of your hóuse;
your chíldren like shóots of the ólive,*
aróund your táble.

Indéed thús shall be bléssed*
the mán who fears the Lórd.
May the Lórd bléss you from Síon*
all the dáys of your lífe!
May you sée your chíldren's chíldren†
in a háppy Jerúsalem!*

On Ísrael, péace!

Ant. May the Lord bless you and may you see peace all the days of your life.
Ant. 3: The Lord will destroy your enemies for you.

THE PEOPLE RENEW THEIR CONFIDENCE IN THE LORD AFTER A TIME OF AFFLICTION PSALM 128(129)

The Church tells of the suffering it endures (St Augustine)

'They have préssed me hárd from my yóuth,'*

this is Israel's sóng.
'They have préssed me hárd from my yóuth*
but could néver destróy me.

They plóughed my báck like plóughmen,*
drawing lóng fúrrows.
But the Lórd who is júst, has destróyed*
the yóke of the wícked.'

Lét them be shámed and róuted,*
thóse who hate Síon!
Lét them be like gráss on the róof*
that wíthers before it flówers.

With thát no réaper fills his árms,*
no bínder makes his shéaves
and thóse passing bý will not sáy:†
('On yóu the Lord's bléssing!'*
'We bléss you in the náme of the Lórd.'

Ant. The Lord will destroy your enemies for you.
Eastertide: Alleluia, alleluia, alleluia.

At the other Hours, the complementary psalms from Series I and II.

Through the Year

Before Noon

SCRIPTURE READING 1 JN 3:23-24

His commandments are these:
that we believe in the name of his Son Jesus Christ
and that we love one another
as he told us to.
Whoever keeps his commandments
lives in God and God lives in him.
We know that he lives in us
by the Spirit that he has given us.
℣ You, Lord, look after the just man.
℟ You, O God, test the mind and the heart.

CONCLUDING PRAYER

Lord, who at this hour
bestowed the gift of the Holy Spirit on the apostles
while they were at prayer,
grant us a share in that same grace.
Through Christ our Lord.

Midday

SCRIPTURE READING WIS 1:1-2

Love virtue, you who are judges on earth,
let honesty prompt your thinking about the Lord,
seek him in simplicity of heart;
since he is to be found by those who do not put him to the test,
he shows himself to those who do not distrust him.
℣ Hope in the Lord and do what is good.
℟ Then you will possess the land and be secure.

CONCLUDING PRAYER

Almighty God,
you are all light,
in you there is no darkness.
Let your light shine upon us in all its radiance,
so that we may walk gladly in the way of your commandments.
Through Christ our Lord.

Afternoon

SCRIPTURE READING HEB 12:1b-2

We should throw off everything that hinders us, especially the sin that clings so easily, and keep running steadily in the race we have started. Let us not lose sight of Jesus, who leads us in our faith and brings it to perfection; for the sake of the joy which was still in the future, he endured the cross, disregarding the shamefulness of it, and from now on has taken his place at the right of God's throne.
℣ My soul is waiting on the Lord.
℟ I count on his word.

CONCLUDING PRAYER

Lord, in answer to our prayer

give us patience in suffering hardships
after the example of your Only-begotten Son,
who lives and reigns for ever and ever.

WEEK 4: FRIDAY

Hymn *(see p. 96)*

PSALMODY

In Advent, Christmastide and Lent the antiphons are proper.

Ant. Eastertide: Alleluia, alleluia, alleluia.
Ant. 1: The lovers of your law have great peace, Lord.

PSALM 118(119):161-168 XXI (SHIN)

Though prínces oppréss me without cáuse*
I stand in áwe of your wórd.
I táke delight in your prómise*
like óne who finds a tréasure.

Líes I háte and detést*
but your láw is my lóve.
Séven times a dáy I práise you*
for your júst decrées.

The lóvers of your láw have great péace;*
they néver stúmble.
I awáit your saving hélp, O Lórd,*
I fulfil your commánds.

My sóul obéys your wíll*
and lóves it déarly.
I obéy your précepts and your wíll;*
all that I dó is befóre you.

Ant. The lovers of your law have great peace, Lord.
Ant. 2: The whole group of believers was united in heart and in soul.

THE JOY OF BROTHERLY UNITY PSALM 132(133)

Let us love one another since love comes from God (1 Jn 4:7)

How góod and how pléasant it ís,*
when bróthers líve in únity!

It is líke precious óil upon the héad*
running dówn upon the béard,
running dówn upon Áaron's béard*
upon the cóllar of his róbes.

It is líke the dew of Hérmon which fálls*
on the héights of Síon.
For thére the Lórd gives his bléssing,*
lífe for éver.

Ant. The whole group of believers was united in heart and in soul.
Ant. 3: Guard me from the hands of the wicked, O Lord, my mighty help.

YOU ARE MY REFUGE PSALM 139(140):1-9,13-14

The Son of Man is to be betrayed into the hands of sinners (Mt 26:45)

Réscue me, Lórd, from evil mén;*
from the víolent kéep me sáfe,
from thóse who plan évil in their héarts*
and stír up strífe every dáy;
who shárpen their tóngue like an ádder's,*
with the póison of víper on their líps.

Lord, guárd me from the hánds of the wícked;†
from the víolent kéep me sáfe;*
they plán to máke me stúmble.
The próud have hídden a tráp,†
have spréad out línes in a nét,*
set snáres acróss my páth.

I have sáid to the Lórd: 'You are my Gód.'*
Lord, héar the crý of my appéal!
Lord my Gód, my míghty hélp,*
you shíeld my héad in the báttle.

Do not gránt the wícked their desíre*
nor lét their plóts succéed.

I know the Lórd will avénge the póor,*
that hé will do jústice for the néedy.
Yes, the júst will práise your náme:*
the úpright shall líve in your présence.

Ant. Guard me from the hands of the wicked, O Lord, my mighty help.
Eastertide: Alleluia, alleluia, alleluia.

At the other Hours, the complementary psalms.

Through the Year

Before Noon

SCRIPTURE READING ROM 12:17a,19b-21

Repay no one evil for evil; for it is written, Vengeance is mine, I will repay, says the Lord. No, if your enemy is hungry, feed him; if he is thirsty, give him drink. Do not be overcome by evil, but overcome evil with good.

℣ The love of the Lord is everlasting.
℟ His justice is for those who keep his commandments.

CONCLUDING PRAYER

Lord Jesus Christ,
at this hour you were led to the cross
to suffer the penalty of death for the salvation of mankind:
in your mercy grant us pardon for our past offences
and by your power preserve us from future falls.
Who live and reign for ever and ever.

Midday

SCRIPTURE READING 1 JN 3:16

This has taught us love –
that he gave up his life for us;
and we, too, ought to give up our lives
for our brothers.

℣ Give thanks to the Lord for he is good.
℟ His great love is without end.

CONCLUDING PRAYER

Lord Jesus Christ,
who at this hour
when the whole world was shrouded in darkness
mounted the wood of the cross
as the innocent victim for our redemption,
give us always that light
which will bring us to eternal life.
Who live and reign for ever and ever.

Afternoon

SCRIPTURE READING 1 JN 4:9-11

God's love for us was revealed
when God sent into the world his only Son
so that we could have life through him;
this is the love I mean:
not our love for God,
but God's love for us when he sent his Son
to be the sacrifice that takes our sins away.
My dear people,
since God has loved us so much,
we too should love one another.
℣ Turn your eyes, O God, our protector.
℟ Look on the face of your anointed.

CONCLUDING PRAYER

Lord Jesus Christ,
who on the cross called the penitent thief into your kingdom,
in faith and trust and confessing our sins
we implore your mercy
that after our death
you will lead us rejoicing through the gates of paradise.
Who live and reign for ever and ever.

WEEK 4: SATURDAY

Hymn *(see p. 96)*

PSALMODY

In Advent, Christmastide and Lent the antiphons are proper.

Ant. Eastertide: Alleluia, alleluia, alleluia.
Ant. 1: Let your hand be ready to help me, since I have chosen your precepts.

PSALM 118(119):169-176 XXII(TAU)

Lórd, let my crý come befóre you:*
téach me by your wórd.
Let my pléading cóme befóre you;*
sáve me by your prómise.

Let my líps procláim your práise*
because you téach me your commánds.
Let my tóngue síng your prómise*
for your commánds are júst.

Let your hánd be réady to hélp me,*
since I have chósen your précepts.
Lord, I lóng for your sáving hélp*
and your láw is my delíght.

Give lífe to my sóul that I may práise you.*
Let your decrées give me hélp.
I am lóst like a shéep; seek your sérvant*
for I remémber your commánds.

Ant. Let your hand be ready to help me, since I have chosen your precepts.
Ant. 2: Your throne, O God, shall endure for ever.

ROYAL WEDDING SONG PSALM 44(45)

Behold, the bridegroom is coming; go out to meet him (Mt 25:6)

I

My héart overflóws with nóble wórds.†
To the kíng I must spéak the sóng I have máde;*
my tóngue as nímble as the pén of a scríbe.

Yóu are the fáirest of the chíldren of mén†
and gráciousness is póured upón your líps:*
because Gód has bléssed you for évermóre.

O míghty one, gírd your swórd upon your thígh;†
in spléndour and státe, ríde on in tríumph*
for the cáuse of trúth and góodness and ríght.

Take aím with your bów in your dréad right hánd.†
Your árrows are shárp: peóples fall benéath you.*
The fóes of the kíng fall dówn and lose héart.

Your thróne, O Gód, shall endúre for éver.†
A scéptre of jústice is the scéptre of your kíngdom.*
Your lóve is for jústice; your hátred for évil.

Therefore Gód, your Gód, has anóinted yóu†
with the óil of gládness abóve other kíngs:*
your róbes are frágrant with áloes and mýrrh.

From the ívory pálace you are gréeted with músic.†
The dáughters of kíngs are amóng your lóved ones.*
On your ríght stands the quéen in góld of Óphir.

Ant. Your throne, O God, shall endure for ever.
Ant. 3: I saw the new Jerusalem, as beautiful as a bride prepared to meet her husband.

II

Lísten, O dáughter, give éar to my wórds:*
forgét your own péople and your fáther's hóuse.
Só will the kíng desíre your béauty:*
Hé is your lórd, pay hómage to hím.

And the péople of Týre shall cóme with gífts,*
the ríchest of the péople shall séek your fávour.
The dáughter of the kíng is clóthed with spléndour,*
her róbes embróidered with péarls set in góld.

She is léd to the kíng with her maíden compánions.†
Théy are escórted amid gládness and jóy;*
they páss withín the pálace of the kíng.

Sóns shall be yóurs in pláce of your fáthers:*
you will máke them prínces over áll the éarth.
May this sóng make your náme for éver remémbered.*
May the péoples práise you from áge to áge.

Ant. I saw the new Jerusalem, as beautiful as a bride prepared to meet her husband.
Eastertide: Alleluia, alleluia, alleluia.

At the other Hours, the complementary psalms.

Through the Year

Before Noon

SCRIPTURE READING DAN 6:26b-27

He is the living God, he endures for ever,
his sovereignty will never be destroyed
and his kingship never end.
He saves, sets free, and works signs and wonders
in the heavens and on earth.
℣ Be still and know that I am God.
℟ I am supreme among the nations, supreme on earth.

CONCLUDING PRAYER

Send forth the light of the holy Spirit on us,
Lord God, almighty Father,
subject as we are to your divine majesty:
so that safe from every foe,
we may always rejoice
as we celebrate your praise.
Through Christ our Lord.

Midday

SCRIPTURE READING ROM 15:5-7

May the God of steadfastness and encouragement grant you to live in such harmony with one another, in accord with Christ Jesus, that together you may with one voice glorify the God and Father of our Lord Jesus Christ. Welcome one another, therefore, as Christ has welcomed you, for the glory of God.

℣ The Lord takes delight in his people.
℟ He crowns the poor with salvation.

CONCLUDING PRAYER

Lord God,
living light of eternal love,
grant that always aglow with charity,
we may love you above all else
and our brethren for your sake,
with one and the self-same love.
Through Christ our Lord.

Afternoon

SCRIPTURE READING PHIL 4:8,9b

My brothers, fill your minds with those things that are good and deserve praise: things that are true, noble, right, pure, lovely, and honourable. And the God who gives us peace will be with you.

℣ I will give you glory, O God my King.
℟ I will bless your name for ever.

CONCLUDING PRAYER

Give us perfect peace, Lord,
so that we may delight in serving you
all the days of our life,
and at the last, with our Lady's help,
come safely to your presence.
Through Christ our Lord.

COMPLEMENTARY PSALMODY FOR PRAYER DURING THE DAY

Before Noon, Midday and Afternoon

℣ O God, come to our aid . . .

HYMN

O blessèd Lord, Creator God,
In you all things are rendered pure,
By you are strengthened to endure.

O blessèd, holy hand of God,
All things are sanctified by you;
Adorned, enriched, you make them new.

O blessèd Majesty of God,
Containing all that you have filled;
All things are done as you have willed.

O blessèd, holy Trinity,
Serene and certain in your ways;
You are the light of endless days.

The hymns for these Hours are set out in the appendix with the appropriate antiphons for each season. The hymn 'O blessed Lord, Creator God,' given above is for use on certain solemnities when these psalms are said for Prayer During the Day. Proper antiphons for particular celebrations are given in the Propers of Seasons and Saints, and in the Common Offices.

Such seasonal and proper antiphons are only said before the first and after the last psalm of each Hour.

SERIES I (BEFORE NOON)

Ant. Eastertide: Alleluia, alleluia, alleluia.
Ant. 1: I called and the Lord answered me.

LONGING FOR PEACE — PSALM 119(120)

Show patience in times of trouble; never cease praying (Rom 12:12)

To the Lórd in the hóur of my distréss*
I cáll and he ánswers me.
'O Lórd, save my sóul from lying líps,*
from the tóngue of the decéitful.'

Whát shall he páy you in retúrn,*
O tréacherous tóngue?
The wárrior's árrows shárpened*
and cóals, red-hot, blázing.

Alas, that I abíde a stránger in Méshech,*
dwell among the ténts of Kédar!

Long enóugh have Í been dwélling*
with thóse who hate péace.
Í am for péace, but when I spéak,*
théy are for fíghting.

Ant. I called and the Lord answered me.
Ant. 2: May the Lord guard your going in and coming out.

GOD, THE PROTECTOR OF HIS PEOPLE — PSALM 120(121)

They will never hunger or thirst again; neither the sun or scorching wind will ever plague them (Rev 7:16)

I líft up my éyes to the móuntains:*
from whére shall come my hélp?
My hélp shall cóme from the Lórd*
who made héaven and éarth.

May he néver allów you to stúmble!*
Let him sléep not, your guárd.
Nó, he sléeps not nor slúmbers,*
Ísrael's guárd.

The Lórd is your guárd and your sháde;*
at your ríght side he stánds.
By dáy the sún shall not smíte you*
nor the móon in the níght.

The Lórd will guárd you from évil,*
he will guárd your sóul.
The Lord will guárd your góing and cóming*
both nów and for éver.

Ant. May the Lord guard your going in and coming out.
Ant. 3: I rejoiced in the things which were said to me.

THE HOLY CITY OF JERUSALEM PSALM 121(122)

You have come to Mount Zion and the city of the living God, the heavenly Jerusalem (Heb 12:22)

I rejóiced when I héard them sáy:*
'Let us gó to God's hóuse.'
And nów our féet are stánding*
within your gátes, O Jerúsalem.

Jerúsalem is buílt as a cíty*
stróngly compáct.
It is thére that the tríbes go úp,*
the tríbes of the Lórd.

For Ísrael's láw it ís,*
there to práise the Lord's náme.
Thére were set the thrónes of júdgment*
of the hóuse of Dávid.

For the péace of Jerúsalem pray:*
'Péace be to your hómes!
May péace réign in your wálls,*
in your pálaces, péace!'

For lóve of my bréthren and fríends*
I say: 'Péace upon yóu!'
For lóve of the hóuse of the Lórd*
I will ásk for your góod.

Ant. I rejoiced in the things which were said to me.
Eastertide: Alleluia, alleluia, alleluia.

The scripture reading and the concluding prayer are from the psalter or one of the Propers or of the Commons according to the season or the celebration.

SERIES II (MIDDAY)

Ant. Eastertide: Alleluia, alleluia, alleluia.
Ant. 1: You, Lord, who dwell in the heavens, have mercy on us.

THE LORD IS THE HOPE OF HIS PEOPLE — PSALM 122(123)

The two blind men cried out, 'Lord, have pity on us, Son of David' (Mt 20:30)

To ýou have I lífted up my éyes,*
you who dwéll in the héavens:
my éyes, like the éyes of sláves*
on the hánd of their lórds.

Líke the éyes of a sérvant*
on the hánd of her místress,
so our éyes are on the Lórd our Gód*
till he shów us his mércy.*

Have mércy on us, Lórd, have mércy.*
We are filled with contémpt.
Indéed all too fúll is our sóul†
with the scórn of the rích,*
with the próud man's disdáin.

Ant. You, Lord, who dwell in the heavens, have mercy on us.
Ant. 2: Our help is in the name of the Lord.

OUR HELP IS IN THE NAME OF THE LORD — PSALM 123(124)

The Lord said to Paul, 'Do not fear; for I am with you' (Acts 18:9-10)

'If the Lórd had not béen on our síde,'*
this is Ísrael's sóng.

'If the Lórd had not béen on our síde*
when mén rose agáinst us,
thén would they have swállowed us alíve*
when their ánger was kíndled.

Thén would the wáters have engúlfed us,*
the tórrent gone óver us;
óver our héad would have swépt*
the ráging wáters.'

Bléssed be the Lórd who did not gíve us*
a préy to their téeth!
Our lífe, like a bírd, has escáped*
from the snáre of the fówler.

Indéed the snáre has been bróken*
and wé have escáped.
Our hélp is in the náme of the Lórd,*
who made héaven and éarth.

Ant. Our help is in the name of the Lord.
Ant. 3: The Lord surrounds his people both now and for ever.

THE LORD, THE PROTECTOR OF HIS PEOPLE — PSALM 124(125)

Peace to the Israel of God (Gal 6:16)

Thóse who put their trúst in the Lórd†
are like Mount Síon, that cánnot be sháken,*
that stánds for éver.

Jerúsalem! The móuntains surróund her,†
so the Lórd surróunds his péople*
both nów and for éver.

For the scéptre of the wícked shall not rést*
over the lánd of the júst
for féar that the hánds of the júst*
should túrn to évil.

Do góod, Lord, to thóse who are góod,*
to the úpright of héart;

but the cróoked and thóse who do évil,*
dríve them awáy!

On Ísrael, péace!

Ant. The Lord surrounds his people both now and for ever.
Eastertide: Alleluia, alleluia, alleluia.

SERIES III (AFTERNOON)

Ant. Eastertide: Alleluia, alleluia, alleluia.
Ant. 1: What marvels the Lord worked for us: indeed we are glad.

JOY AND HOPE IN GOD PSALM 125(126)

Just as you are sharing in our sufferings, so also will you share our consolations (2 Cor 1:7)

When the Lórd delivered Síon from bóndage,*
It séemed like a dréam.
Thén was our móuth filled with láughter,*
on our líps there were sóngs.

The héathens themsélves said: 'What márvels*
the Lórd worked for thém!'
What márvels the Lórd worked for ús!*
Indéed we were glád.

Delíver us, O Lórd, from our bóndage*
as stréams in dry lánd.
Thóse who are sówing in téars*
will síng when they réap.

They go óut, they go óut, full of téars,*
carrying séed for the sówing:
they come báck, they come báck, full of sóng,*
cárrying their shéaves.

Ant. What marvels the Lord worked for us: indeed we are glad.
Ant. 2: The Lord will build the house for us; he will watch over our city.

SUCCESS DEPENDS ON THE LORD'S BLESSING PSALM 126(127)

You are God's building (1 Cor 3:9)

If the Lórd does not buíld the hóuse,*
in váin do its buílders lábour;
if the Lórd does not wátch over the cíty,*
in váin does the wátchman keep vígil.

In váin is your éarlier rísing,*
your góing láter to rést,
you who tóil for the bréad you éat:*
when he pours gífts on his belóved while they slúmber.

Truly sóns are a gíft from the Lórd,*
a bléssing, the frúit of the wómb.
Indéed the sóns of yóuth*
are like árrows in the hánd of a wárrior.

Ó the háppiness of the mán*
who has filled his quíver with these árrows!
Hé will have no cáuse for sháme*
when he dispútes with his fóes in the gáteways.

Ant. The Lord will build the house for us; he will watch over our city.
Ant. 3: O blessed are those who fear the Lord.†

PEACE IN THE HOME, A GIFT FROM THE LORD PSALM 127(128)

'May the Lord bless you from Sion', that is, from his Church (Arnobius)

O bléssed are thóse who fear the Lórd*
†and wálk in his wáys!

By the lábour of your hánds you shall éat.*
You will be háppy and prósper;
your wífe like a frúitful víne*
in the héart of your hóuse;
your chíldren like shóots of the ólive,*
aróund your táble.

Indéed thús shall be bléssed*
the mán who fears the Lórd.
May the Lórd bléss you from Síon*
all the dáys of your lífe!
May you sée your chíldren's chíldren*
in a háppy Jerúsalem!

On Ísrael, péace!

Ant. O blessed are those who fear the Lord.
Eastertide: Alleluia, alleluia, alleluia.

THE PROPER OF SEASONS

A selection of texts is given in the pages that follow to enable the user to advert to the season of the year. For the full variety of seasonal texts offered by the Liturgy of the Hours, see The Divine Office *or* Daily Prayer.

Unless otherwise indicated, the psalmody is as given in the Four Week Psalter. The hymn in the Psalter, or a hymn suitable to the season and to the time of day should be chosen.

ADVENT SUNDAYS 1-4

ANTIPHON

Before Noon: The prophets foretold that the Saviour would be born of the Virgin Mary.

Midday: The angel Gabriel said to Mary, 'Rejoice, most highly favoured one! The Lord is with you. Of all women you are the most blessed.'

Afternoon: Mary was greatly troubled at this greeting and wondered what it might mean. She said, 'I am to give birth to a King without ceasing to be a virgin.'

These antiphons are said all through Advent and are chosen according to the time of day, if only one Hour is said. Proper antiphons replace those given with the psalms in the psalter for these Hours, and are said only before the first and after the last psalm of each Hour.

PSALMS

Psalms as in the Psalter for the relevant week. Where more than one of the Hours is said, the complementary psalms are used *(see p. 00).*

SCRIPTURE READING

Before Noon ROM 13:13-14a

Let us conduct ourselves properly, as people who live in the light of day; no orgies or drunkenness, no immorality or indecency, no fighting or jealousy. But take up the weapons of the Lord Jesus Christ.

℣ The nations shall fear your name, Lord.

℟ And all the kings of the earth your glory.

Midday 1 THESS 3:12-13

May the Lord be generous in increasing your love and make you love one another and the whole human race as much as we love you. And may he so confirm your hearts in holiness that you may be blameless in the sight of our God and Father when our Lord Jesus Christ comes with all his saints.

℣ Remember us, Lord, for the love you bear your people.

℟ Come to us as a Saviour.

Afternoon Cf 2 THESS 1:6,7,10

God will very rightly repay with injury those who are injuring you, and reward you, who are suffering now, with the same peace as he will give us, when the Lord Jesus appears from heaven with the angels of his power; on that day when he comes to be glorified among his saints and seen in his glory by all who believe in him.

℣ Come, Lord, and make no delay.
℟ Release your people from their sin.

CONCLUDING PRAYER

Sunday 1: Grant, almighty Father,
that when Christ comes again
we may go out to meet him,
bearing the harvest of good works
achieved by your grace.
We pray that he will receive us into the company of the saints
and call us into the kingdom of heaven.
Through Christ our Lord.

Sunday 2: Almighty and merciful God,
let neither our daily work nor the cares of this life
prevent us from hastening to meet your Son.
Enlighten us with your wisdom,
and lead us into his company.
Through Christ our Lord.

Sunday 3: Grant, almighty God, that looking forward in faith
to the feast of our Lord's birth,
we may feel all the happiness our Saviour brings,
and celebrate his coming with unfailing joy.
Through Christ our Lord.

Sunday 4: Lord, open our hearts to your grace.
Through the angel's message to Mary
we have learned to believe
in the incarnation of Christ your Son.
Lead us by his passion and cross
to the glory of his resurrection.
Through Christ our Lord.

MONDAYS OF ADVENT

Before Noon

Ant. The prophets foretold that the Saviour would be born of the Virgin Mary.

SCRIPTURE READING Cf IS 10:20-21

In that day the remnant of Israel and the survivors of the house of Jacob will lean upon the Lord, the Holy One of Israel, in truth. A remnant will return, the remnant of Jacob, to the mighty God.

℣ The nations shall fear your name, Lord.
℟ And all the kings of the earth your glory.

Midday

Ant. The angel Gabriel said to Mary, 'Rejoice, most highly favoured one! The Lord is with you. Of all women you are the most blessed.'

SCRIPTURE READING Cf IS 10:24,27

Thus says the Lord, the Lord of hosts: 'O my people who dwell in Zion, be not afraid. In that day the burden will depart from your shoulder and the yoke from your neck.'

℣ Remember us, Lord, for the love you bear your people.
℟ Come to us as a Saviour.

Afternoon

Ant. Mary was greatly troubled at this greeting and wondered what it might mean. She said, 'I am to give birth to a King without ceasing to be a virgin.'

SCRIPTURE READING Cf IS 13:22;14:1

His time is close at hand, and his days will not be prolonged. The Lord will have compassion on Jacob and Israel will be saved.

℣ Come, Lord, and make no delay.
℟ Release your people from their sin.

CONCLUDING PRAYER

Give us the grace, Lord,
to be ever on the watch for Christ, your Son.

When he comes and knocks at our door,
let him find us alert in prayer,
joyfully proclaiming his glory.
Through Christ our Lord.

TUESDAYS OF ADVENT

Before Noon

Ant. The prophets foretold that the Saviour would be born of the Virgin Mary.

SCRIPTURE READING JER 23:5

The days are now coming, says the Lord, when I will make a righteous Branch spring for David's line, a king who shall rule wisely, maintaining law and justice in the land.

℣ The nations shall fear your name, Lord.
℟ And all the kings of the earth your glory.

Midday

Ant. The angel Gabriel said to Mary, 'Rejoice, most highly favoured one! The Lord is with you. Of all women you are the most blessed.'

SCRIPTURE READING JER 23:6

In his days Judah shall be kept safe, and Israel shall live undisturbed. This is the name to be given to him: The Lord is our Righteousness.

℣ Remember us, Lord, for the love you bear your people.
℟ Come to us as a Saviour.

Afternoon

Ant. Mary was greatly troubled at this greeting and wondered what it might mean. She said, 'I am to give birth to a King without ceasing to be a virgin.'

SCRIPTURE READING EZEK 34:15-16

I myself will pasture my sheep, I myself will show them where to rest – it is the Lord God who speaks. I shall look for the lost one, bring back the stray, bandage the wounded and make the weak strong. I shall be a true

shepherd to them.
℣ Come, Lord, and make no delay.
℟ Release your people from their sin.

CONCLUDING PRAYER

Take pity on our distress, Lord God:
show us your love.
May the coming of your Son strengthen us
and cleanse us from all trace of sin.
Through Christ our Lord.

WEDNESDAYS OF ADVENT

Before Noon

Ant. The prophets foretold that the Saviour would be born of the Virgin Mary.

SCRIPTURE READING IS 2:11

Human pride will lower its eyes, the arrogance of men will be humbled. The Lord alone shall be exalted in that day.
℣ The nations shall fear your name, Lord.
℟ And all the kings of the earth your glory.

Midday

Ant. The angel Gabriel said to Mary, 'Rejoice, most highly favoured one! The Lord is with you. Of all women you are the most blessed.'

SCRIPTURE READING IS 12:2

Behold, God is my salvation;
I will trust, and will not be afraid;
for the Lord God is my strength and my song,
and he has become my salvation.
℣ Remember us, Lord, for the love you bear your people.
℟ Come to us as a Saviour.

Afternoon

Ant. Mary was greatly troubled at this greeting and wondered what it might mean. She said, 'I am going to give birth to a King without ceasing to be a virgin.'

SCRIPTURE READING DAN 9:19

O Lord, hear; O Lord, forgive; O Lord, give heed and act; delay not, for your own sake, O my God, because your city and your people are called by your name.

℣ Come, Lord, and make no delay.
℟ Release your people from their sin.

CONCLUDING PRAYER

Prepare our hearts, Lord,
by the power of your grace.
When Christ comes,
may he find us worthy
to receive from his hand the bread of heaven
at the feast of eternal life.
Through Christ our Lord.

THURSDAYS OF ADVENT

Before Noon

Ant. The prophets foretold that the Saviour would be born of the Virgin Mary.

SCRIPTURE READING MIC 5:4-5a

He will stand and feed his flock with the power of the Lord, with the majesty of the name of his God. They will live secure, for from then on he will extend his power to the ends of the land. He himself will be peace.

℣ The nations shall fear your name, Lord.
℟ And all the kings of the earth your glory.

Midday

Ant. The angel Gabriel said to Mary, 'Rejoice, most highly favoured one! The Lord is with you. Of all women you are the most blessed.'

SCRIPTURE READING HAG 2:6,9

A little while now, and I am going to shake the heavens and the earth, the sea and the dry land. The new glory of this Temple is going to surpass the old, says the Lord of Hosts, and in this place I will give peace.

℣ Remember us, Lord, for the love you bear your people.
℟ Come to us as a Saviour.

Afternoon

Ant. Mary was greatly troubled at this greeting and wondered what it might mean. She said, 'I am to give birth to a King without ceasing to be a virgin.'

SCRIPTURE READING MAL 4:2

For you who fear my name, the sun of righteousness shall rise with healing in his wings, says the Lord of Hosts.

℣ Come, Lord, and make no delay.
℟ Release your people from their sin.

CONCLUDING PRAYER

Show forth your power, Lord, and come.
Come in your great strength and help us.
Be merciful and forgiving,
and hasten the salvation which only our sins delay.
Through Christ our Lord.

FRIDAYS OF ADVENT

Before Noon

Ant. The prophets foretold that the Saviour would be born of the Virgin Mary.

SCRIPTURE READING JER 29:11,13

I know the plans I have for you, says the Lord, plans for welfare and not for evil, to give you a future and a hope. You will seek me and find me when you seek me with all your heart.

℣ The nations shall fear your name, Lord.
℟ And all the kings of the earth your glory.

Midday

Ant. The angel Gabriel said to Mary, 'Rejoice, most highly favoured one! The Lord is with you. Of all women you are the most blessed.'

SCRIPTURE READING JER 30:18

These are the words of the Lord:
Watch; I will restore the fortunes of Jacob's clans
and show my love for all his dwellings.
℣ Remember us, Lord, for the love you bear your people.
℟ Come to us as a Saviour.

Afternoon

Ant. Mary was greatly troubled at this greeting and wondered what it might mean. She said, 'I am to give birth to a King without ceasing to be a virgin.'

SCRIPTURE READING BAR 3:5-6a

Do not recall the misdeeds of our fathers, but remember now your power and your name, for you are the Lord our God.
℣ Come, Lord, and make no delay.
℟ Release your people from their sin.

CONCLUDING PRAYER

Call forth your power, Lord;
come and save us from the judgment
that threatens us by reason of our sins.
Come, and set us free.
Through Christ our Lord.

SATURDAYS OF ADVENT

Before Noon

Ant. The prophets foretold that the Saviour would be born of the Virgin Mary.

SCRIPTURE READING IS 4:2

On that day the plant that the Lord has grown
shall become glorious in its beauty,
and the fruit of the land shall be
the pride and splendour
of the survivors of Israel.

℣ The nations shall fear your name, Lord.
℟ And all the kings of the earth your glory.

Midday

Ant. The angel Gabriel said to Mary, 'Rejoice, most highly favoured one! The Lord is with you. Of all women you are the most blessed.'

SCRIPTURE READING IS 4:3

Those who are left in Zion, who remain in Jerusalem, every one enrolled in the book of life, shall be called holy.

℣ Remember us, Lord, for the love you bear your people.
℟ Come to us as a Saviour.

Afternoon

Ant. Mary was greatly troubled at this greeting and wondered what it might mean. She said, 'I am to give birth to a King without ceasing to be a virgin.'

SCRIPTURE READING IS 61:11

For as the earth puts forth her blossom or bushes in the garden burst into flower, so shall the Lord God make righteousness and praise blossom before all the nations.

℣ Come, Lord, and make no delay.
℟ Release your people from their sin.

CONCLUDING PRAYER

Lord, to free man from his sinful state
you sent your only Son into this world.
Grant to us who in faith and love wait for his coming
your gift of grace
and the reward of true freedom.
Through Christ our Lord.

SEASON OF CHRISTMAS

Christmay Day

THE NATIVITY OF OUR LORD JESUS CHRIST

Solemnity

ANTIPHON

Before Noon: Joseph and Mary, the mother of Jesus, wondered at what was being said about him.

Midday: Mary treasured all these things and pondered them in her heart.

Afternoon: My eyes have seen the salvation which you prepared in the presence of all the peoples.

Psalm 18(19)B, Psalter, Week 1, Monday, p. 13.

THE LORD IS THE KING OF ALL PSALM 46(47)

He is seated at the right hand of the Father, and his kingdom will have no end

All péoples, cláp your hánds,*
cry to Gód with shóuts of jóy!
For the Lórd, the Most Hígh, we must féar,*
great kíng over áll the éarth.

He subdúes péoples únder us*
and nátions únder our féet.
Our inhéritance, our glóry, is from hím,*
gíven to Jácob out of lóve.

God goes úp with shóuts of jóy;*
the Lord ascénds with trúmpet blást.
Sing práise for Gód, sing práise,*
sing práise to our kíng, sing práise.

God is kíng of áll the éarth,*
Sing práise with áll your skíll.
God is kíng óver the nátions;*

God réigns on his hóly thróne.

The prínces of the péoples are assémbled*
with the péople of Ábraham's Gód.
The rúlers of the éarth belong to Gód,*
to Gód who réigns over áll.

THANKSGIVING FOR THE SALVATION OF GOD'S PEOPLE PSALM 47(48)

He took me to the top of a great mountain, and showed me the holy city of Jerusalem (Rev 21:10)

The Lord is gréat and wórthy to be práised*
in the cíty of our Gód.
†His holy móuntain ríses in béauty,*
the jóy of all the éarth.

Mount Síon, true póle of the éarth,*
the Gréat King's cíty!
Gód, in the mídst of its cítadels,*
has shówn himself its strónghold.

For the kíngs assémbled togéther,*
togéther they advánced.
They sáw; at ónce they were astóunded;*
dismáyed, they fled in féar.

A trémbling séized them thére,*
like the pángs of bírth,
By the éast wind yóu have destróyed*
the shíps of Thársis.

As we have héard, só we have séen*
in the cíty of our Gód,
in the cíty of the Lórd of hósts*
which Gód upholds for éver.

O Gód, we pónder your lóve*
withín your témple.
Your práise, O Gód, like your náme*
reaches the énds of the éarth.

With jústice your ríght hand is fílled.*
Mount Síon rejóices;
the péople of Júdah rejóice*
at the síght of your júdgments.

Walk through Síon, wálk all róund it;*
count the númber of its tówers.
Revíew áll its rámparts,*
exámine its cástles,

that you may téll the néxt generátion*
that súch is our Gód,
our Gód for éver and álways.*
It is hé who léads us.

Before Noon

Ant. Joseph and Mary, the mother of Jesus, wondered at what was being said about him.

SCRIPTURE READING TIT 2:11-12

The grace of God has appeared for the salvation of all men, training us to renounce irreligion and worldly passions, and to live sober, upright, and godly lives in this world.

℣ The Lord has remembered his loving mercy, alleluia.
℟ He has kept faith with the house of Israel, alleluia.

Midday

Ant. Mary treasured all these things and pondered them in her heart.

SCRIPTURE READING 1 JN 4:9

God's love for us was revealed when God sent into the world his only Son so that we could have life through him.

℣ All the ends of the earth stand in awe, alleluia.
℟ They have seen the saving power of our God, alleluia.

Afternoon

Ant. My eyes have seen the salvation which you prepared in the presence of all the peoples.

SCRIPTURE READING ACTS 10:36

God sent his word to the Israelites and gave the good news of peace through Jesus Christ, who is Lord of all.

℣ Mercy and faithfulness have met, alleluia.
℟ Justice and peace have embraced, alleluia.

CONCLUDING PRAYER

God, our Father,
our human nature is the wonderful work of your hands,
made still more wonderful by your work of redemption.
Your Son took to himself our manhood,
grant us a share in the godhead of Jesus Christ,
who lives and reigns for ever and ever.

Sunday within the Octave of Christmas

FEAST OF THE HOLY FAMILY

Psalter: Week 1

The psalms are taken from Sunday, Week 1, pp. 9 ff.

When this feast is celebrated on a weekday, the psalms are of the day as in the psalter. When the complementary psalms are used, Ps 121 may be replaced by Ps 128, p. 112, and Ps 126 by Ps 130 (Tuesday Evening Prayer, Week 3).

Before Noon

Ant. Joseph and Mary, the mother of Jesus, wondered at what was being said about him.

SCRIPTURE READING COL 3:12-13

You are God's chosen people, holy and well beloved, the livery you wear must be tender compassion, kindness, humility, gentleness and patience; you must bear with one another's faults, be generous to each other, where somebody has given grounds for complaint; the Lord's generosity to you must be the model of yours.

℣ The Lord will teach us his ways.
℟ We will walk in his paths.

Midday

Ant. Mary treasured all these things and pondered them in her heart.

SCRIPTURE READING COL 3:14-15

To crown all, charity; that is the bond which makes us perfect. So may the peace of Christ, the very condition of your calling as members of a single body, reign in your hearts. Learn, too, to be grateful.

℣ Ever since my youth, need and sorrow have been my lot.

℟ I have been lifted up only to be cast down and left bewildered.

Afternoon

Ant. My eyes have seen the salvation which you prepared in the presence of all the peoples.

SCRIPTURE READING COL 3:17

Whatever you are doing, whether you speak or act, do everything in the name of the Lord Jesus, giving thanks to God the Father through him.

℣ The Lord will give instruction to all your sons.

℟ He will give peace abundantly to all your children.

CONCLUDING PRAYER

God, our Father,
in the Holy Family of Nazareth
you have given us the true model of a Christian home.
Grant that by following Jesus, Mary, and Joseph
in their love for each other and in the example of their family life
we may come to your home of peace and joy.
Through Christ our Lord.

WEEKDAYS DURING THE CHRISTMAS SEASON

Psalms of the occurring weekday.

Before Noon

Ant. Joseph and Mary, the mother of Jesus, wondered at what was being said about him.

SCRIPTURE READING DEUT 4:7

What great nation is there that has a god so near to it as the Lord our God is to us, whenever we call upon him?

℣ The Lord has remembered his loving mercy, alleluia.
℟ He has kept faith with the house of Israel, alleluia.

Midday

Ant. Mary treasured all these things and pondered them in her heart.

SCRIPTURE READING IS 12:5-6

Sing in honour of the great deeds the Lord has done, make them known for all the world to hear. Cry aloud in praise, people of Zion; great is the Holy One of Israel, that dwells among you.

℣ All the ends of the earth stand in awe, alleluia.
℟ They have seen the saving power of our God, alleluia.

Afternoon

Ant. My eyes have seen the salvation which you prepared in the presence of all the peoples.

SCRIPTURE READING TOB 14:8-9

The Gentiles shall leave their idols, and shall come into Jerusalem, and shall dwell in it. And all the kings of the earth shall rejoice in it, adoring the King of Israel.

℣ Mercy and faithfulness have met, alleluia.
℟ Justice and peace have embraced, alleluia.

CONCLUDING PRAYER

Almighty God and Father,
the human birth of your Only-begotten Son
was the beginning of new life.
May he set us free from the tyranny of sin.
Through Christ our Lord.

1 January
Octave Day of Christmas

SOLEMNITY OF MARY, MOTHER OF GOD

The psalms are taken from the complementary psalms, except on a Sunday. Ps 121 may be replaced by Ps 128, *p. 112* *and Ps 126 by Ps 130 (Tuesday Evening Prayer, Week 3).*

Before Noon

Ant. Joseph and Mary, the mother of Jesus, wondered at what was being said about him.

SCRIPTURE READING ZEPH 3:14,15b

Sing aloud, O daughter of Zion;
shout, O Israel!
Rejoice and exult with all your heart, O daughter of Jerusalem!
The King of Israel, the Lord, is in your midst.
℣ The Lord has remembered his loving mercy, alleluia.
℟ He has kept faith with the house of Israel, alleluia.

Midday

Ant. Mary treasured all these things and pondered them in her heart.

SCRIPTURE READING ZECH 9:9a

Rejoice heart and soul, daughter of Zion!
Shout with gladness, daughter of Jerusalem!
See now, your king comes to you; he is victorious, he is triumphant.
℣ All the ends of the earth stand in awe, alleluia.
℟ They have seen the saving power of our God, alleluia.

Afternoon

Ant. My eyes have seen the salvation which you prepared in the presence of all the peoples.

SCRIPTURE READING BAR 5:3-4

In you God will manifest the splendour of his presence, for the whole world to see; and the name by which he will call you for ever is, Loyalty

rewarded, Piety crowned.
℣ Mercy and faithfulness have met, alleluia.
℟ Justice and peace have embraced, alleluia.

CONCLUDING PRAYER

God, our Father,
since you gave mankind a saviour through blessed Mary,
virgin and mother,
grant that we may feel the power of her intercession
when she pleads for us with Jesus Christ, your Son,
the author of life,
who lives and reigns for ever and ever.

6 January or Sunday between 2 and 8 January

THE EPIPHANY OF THE LORD

Solemnity

ANTIPHON

Before Noon: The mystery, which was hidden from earlier ages and generations, is now made clear.
Midday: Christ came and preached peace to you who were far off, and peace to you who were near.
Afternoon: I have appointed you to be a light to all peoples, to be my saving power to the very ends of the earth.

Psalm 46(47) (Wednesday Morning Prayer, Week 1).

PSALM 85(86):1-10

Turn your éar, O Lórd, and give ánswer*
for Í am póor and néedy.
Preserve my life, for Í am fáithful:*
save the sérvant who trústs in yóu.

You are my Gód, have mércy on me, Lórd,*
for I crý to you áll the day lóng.
Give jóy to your sérvant, O Lórd,*
for to yóu I líft up my sóul.

O Lórd, you are góod and forgíving,*
full of lóve to áll who cáll.

Give héed, O Lórd, to my práyer*
and atténd to the sóund of my vóice.

In the dáy of distréss I will cáll*
and súrely yóu will replý.
Among the góds there is nóne like you, O Lórd;*
nor wórk to compáre with yoúrs.

All the nátions shall cóme to adóre you*
and glórify your náme, O Lórd:
for you are gréat and do márvellous déeds,*
yóu who alóne are Gód.

THE LORD IS VICTOR AND A JUST RULER — PSALM 97(98)

Síng a new sóng to the Lórd*
for hé has worked wónders.
His ríght hand and his hóly árm*
have brought salvátion.

The Lórd has made knówn his salvátion;*
has shown his jústice to the nátions.
He has remémbered his trúth and lóve*
for the hóuse of Ísrael.

All the énds of the éarth have séen*
the salvátion of our Gód.
Shóut to the Lórd all the éarth,*
ríng out your jóy.

Sing psálms to the Lórd with the hárp*
with the sóund of músic.
With trúmpets and the sóund of the hórn*
acclaim the Kíng, the Lórd.

Let the séa and all withín it, thúnder;*
the wórld, and all its péoples.
Let the rívers cláp their hánds*
and the hílls ring out their jóy.

Rejóice at the présence of the Lórd,*
for he comes to rúle the éarth.

He will rúle the wórld with jústice*
and the péoples with fáirness.

Before Noon

Ant. The mystery, which was hidden from earlier ages and generations, is now made clear.

SCRIPTURE READING — REV 15:4

Who will not fear you, Lord?
Who will refuse to declare your greatness?
For you alone are holy.
All the nations will come
And worship before you.
℣ He appeared on earth.
℟ And he lived among men.

Midday

Ant. Christ came and preached peace to you who were far off, and peace to you who were near.

SCRIPTURE READING — IS 49:6

It is too light a thing that you should be my servant
to raise up the tribes of Jacob
and to restore the preserved of Israel;
I will give you as a light to the nations,
that my salvation may reach to the end of the earth.
℣ All the peoples have seen your Holy One.
℟ All the kings have seen your glory.

Afternoon

Ant. I have appointed you to be a light to all peoples, to be my saving power to the very ends of the earth.

SCRIPTURE READING — ZECH 2:11

Many nations shall come over to the Lord on that day and become his people, and he will make his dwelling with you. Then you shall know that the Lord of Hosts has sent me to you.
℣ All peoples, bless our God.
℟ Cry out in praise of him.

CONCLUDING PRAYER

On this day, Lord God,
by a guiding star you revealed your Only-begotten Son
to all the peoples of the world.
Lead us from the faith by which we know you now
to the vision of your glory, face to face.
Through Christ our Lord.

Sunday After 6 January

THE BAPTISM OF THE LORD

Feast

If the Sunday is 7 or 8 January, the Feast of the Baptism is omitted.

The psalms are those of Sunday, Week 3, pp. 67 ff, unless this Sunday falls on 7 January, when those of Sunday, Week 2, pp. 38 ff are used.

Before Noon

Ant. John would have prevented Jesus saying: I need to be baptized by you, and do you come to me?

SCRIPTURE READING IS 11:1-2

A shoot shall grow from the stock of Jesse, and a branch shall spring from his roots. The spirit of the Lord shall rest upon him, a spirit of wisdom and understanding, a spirit of counsel and power, a spirit of knowledge and the fear of the Lord.

℣ He must increase.
℟ But I must decrease.

Midday

Ant. Jesus answered him: Let it be so now; for thus it is fitting for us to fulfil all righteousness.

SCRIPTURE READING IS 52:1

Behold my servant, whom I uphold,
my chosen, in whom my soul delights;
I have put my Spirit upon him,

he will bring forth justice to the nations.
℣ Behold my servant, whom I uphold.
℟ My chosen, in whom my soul delights.

Afternoon

Ant. John bore witness: I saw the Spirit descend as a dove from heaven, and it remained on him.

SCRIPTURE READING — IS 49:6

It is too light a thing that you should be my servant
to raise up the tribes of Jacob
and to restore the preserved of Israel;
I will give you as a light to the nations,
that my salvation may reach to the end of the earth.
℣ I have put my Spirit upon him.
℟ He will bring forth justice to the nations.

CONCLUDING PRAYER

Almighty, ever-living God,
when Christ was baptized in the river Jordan
the Holy Spirit came upon him
and your voice proclaimed from heaven 'This is my beloved Son.'
Grant that we,
who by water and the Holy Spirit are your adopted children,
may continue steadfast in your love.
Through Christ our Lord.

SEASON OF LENT

SUNDAYS OF LENT

Sundays 1 and 5: Psalter Week 1
Sunday 2: Psalter Week 2
Sunday 3: Psalter Week 3
Sunday 4: Psalter Week 4

Before Noon

Ant. This is the time of repentance for us to atone for our sins and seek salvation.

SCRIPTURE READING 1 THESS 4:1-7

Brothers, you learned from us how you should live in order to please God; and now we beg and urge you, in the name of the Lord Jesus, to do even more. God did not call us to live in immorality, but in holiness.

℣ A pure heart create for me, O God.
℟ Put a steadfast spirit within me.

Midday

Ant. As I live, says the Lord, I have no pleasure in the death of the wicked man, rather let him turn from his evil way and live.

SCRIPTURE READING IS 30:15,18

Thus said the Lord God, the Holy One of Israel: in returning and rest you shall be saved; in quietness and trust shall be your strength. Therefore, the Lord waits to be gracious to you; therefore he exalts himself to show mercy to you, for the Lord is a God of justice; blessed are all those who wait for him.

℣ From my sins turn away your face.
℟ And blot out all my guilt.

Afternoon

Ant. Armed with the justice which is the power of God, let us prove ourselves with great patience.

SCRIPTURE READING DEUT 4:29-31

You will seek the Lord your God, and you will find him, if you search after him with all your heart and with all your soul. When you are in tribulation, and all these things come upon you in the latter days, you will return to the Lord your God and obey his voice, for the Lord your God is a merciful God; he will not fail you or destroy you or forget the covenant with your fathers which he swore to them.

℣ My sacrifice is a contrite spirit.
℟ A humbled, contrite heart you will not spurn, O God.

CONCLUDING PRAYER

Through our annual Lenten observance, Lord,
deepen our understanding of the mystery of Christ
and make it a reality in the conduct of our lives.
Through Christ our Lord.

MONDAYS OF LENT

Before Noon

Ant. This the time of repentance for us to atone for our sins and seek salvation.

SCRIPTURE READING WIS 11:24-25

You are merciful to all, Lord, because you can do all things and overlook men's sins so that they can repent. Yes, you love all that exists, you hold nothing of what you have made in abhorrence.

℣ A pure heart create for me, O God.
℟ Put a steadfast spirit within me.

Midday

Ant. As I live, says the Lord, I have no pleasure in the death of the wicked man, rather let him turn from his evil way and live.

SCRIPTURE READING EZEK 18:23

Am I likely to take pleasure in the death of a wicked man, it is the Lord God who speaks, and not prefer to see him renounce his wickedness and live?

℣ From my sins turn away your face.
℟ And blot out all my guilt.

Afternoon
Ant. Armed with the justice which is the power of God, let us prove ourselves with great patience.

SCRIPTURE READING IS 58:7
Share your bread with the hungry, and shelter the homeless poor; clothe the man you see to be naked, and do not turn from your own kin.
℣ My sacrifice is a contrite spirit.
℟ A humbled, contrite heart you will not spurn, O God.

CONCLUDING PRAYER
Turn our hearts back to you, God our Saviour;
form us by your heavenly teaching,
so that we may truly profit by our Lenten observance.
Through Christ our Lord.

TUESDAYS OF LENT

Before Noon
Ant. This is the time of repentance for us to atone for our sins and seek salvation.

SCRIPTURE READING JOEL 2:17
The priests that wait upon the Lord make lament between porch and altar, crying aloud: Spare your people, Lord, spare them; your chosen people, do not put them to the shame of obeying heathen masters.
℣ A pure heart create for me, O God.
℟ Put a steadfast spirit within me.

Midday
Ant. As I live, says the Lord, I have no pleasure in the death of the wicked man, rather let him turn from his evil way and live.

SCRIPTURE READING JER 3:25b

Sinners from our youth upwards, we and our fathers before us, against the Lord our God; the Lord our God, and we would not listen to his voice.

℣ From my sins turn away your face.

℟ And blot out all my guilt.

Afternoon

Ant. Armed with the justice which is the power of God, let us prove ourselves with great patience.

SCRIPTURE READING IS 58:1-2

Shout for all you are worth, raise your voice like a trumpet. Proclaim their faults to my people, their sins to the House of Jacob. They seek me day after day, they long to know my ways, like a nation that wants to act with integrity, and not ignore the law of its God.

℣ My sacrifice is a contrite spirit.

℟ A humbled, contrite heart you will not spurn, O God.

CONCLUDING PRAYER

Look with favour on your family, Lord,
and as at this time we restrain the desires of the body
may our hearts burn with love of you.
Through Christ our Lord.

WEDNESDAYS OF LENT

Before Noon

Ant. This is the time of repentance for us to atone for our sins and seek salvation.

SCRIPTURE READING EZEK 18:30b-32

Repent, renounce all your sins, avoid all occasions of sin! Shake off all the sins you have committed against me, and make yourselves a new heart and a new spirit! Why are you so anxious to die, house of Israel? I take no pleasure in the death of anyone – it is the Lord God who speaks. Repent and live!

℣ A pure heart create for me, O God.
℟ Put a steadfast spirit within me.

Midday

Ant. As I live, says the Lord, I have no pleasure in the death of the wicked man, rather let him turn from his evil way and live.

SCRIPTURE READING ZECH 1:3b-4b

Return to me and I will return to you, says the Lord of Hosts. Do not be like your ancestors, to whom the prophets in the past cried: Turn back from your evil ways and your evil deeds.
℣ From my sins turn away your face.
℟ And blot out all my guilt.

Afternoon

Ant. Armed with the justice which is the power of God, let us prove ourselves with great patience.

SCRIPTURE READING DAN 4:24b

With almsgiving, with mercy to the poor, for your fault and wrong-doing make amends; it may be God will condone your guilt.
℣ My sacrifice is a contrite spirit.
℟ A humbled, contrite heart you will not spurn, O God.

CONCLUDING PRAYER

Look with favour on our Lenten observance, Lord,
and while we subdue our bodies by self-denial,
renew our spirit with the grace that prompts us to good works.
Through Christ our Lord.

THURSDAYS OF LENT

Before Noon

Ant. This is the time of repentance for us to atone for our sins and seek salvation.

SCRIPTURE READING IS 55:6-7

Seek the Lord while he is still to be found, call to him while he is still near. Let the wicked man abandon his way, the evil man his thoughts. Let him turn back to the Lord who will take pity on him, to our God, who is rich in forgiving.

℣ A pure heart create for me, O God.

℟ Put a steadfast spirit within me.

Midday

Ant. As I live, says the Lord, I have no pleasure in the death of the wicked man, rather let him turn from his evil way and live.

SCRIPTURE READING DEUT 30:2-3a

When you return to the Lord your God, you and your children, and obey his voice in all that I command you this day, with all your heart and with all your soul, then the Lord your God will restore your fortunes and have compassion upon you.

℣ From my sins turn away your face.

℟ And blot out all my guilt.

Afternoon

Ant. Armed with the justice which is the power of God, let us prove ourselves with great patience.

SCRIPTURE READING HEB 10:35-36

Do not throw away your confidence, for it carries a great reward. You need endurance if you are to do God's will and win what he has promised.

℣ My sacrifice is a contrite spirit.

℟ A humbled, contrite heart you will not spurn, O God.

CONCLUDING PRAYER

In your bounty, Lord,
give us the Spirit
who alone can teach us to think and do what is right,
so that we, who without you cannot exist,
may live in loving obedience to your will.
Through Christ our Lord.

FRIDAYS OF LENT

Before Noon

Ant. This is the time of repentance for us to atone for our sins and seek salvation.

SCRIPTURE READING IS 55:3

Come to me and listen to my words, hear me, and you shall have life: I will make a covenant with you, this time for ever, to love you faithfully as I loved David.

℣ A pure heart create for me, O God.
℟ Put a steadfast spirit within me.

Midday

Ant. As I live, says the Lord, I have no pleasure in the death of the wicked man, rather let him turn from his evil way and live.

SCRIPTURE READING JER 3:12,14a

Come back to me, the Lord says, and there shall be no frown of mine awaiting you; I am merciful, and vengeance shall not last for ever. Wandering hearts, the Lord bids you come back to him.

℣ From my sins turn away your face.
℟ And blot out all my guilt.

Afternoon

Ant. Armed with the justice which is the power of God, let us prove ourselves with great patience.

SCRIPTURE READING JAS 1:27

The kind of religion which is without stain or fault in the sight of God our Father is this: to go to the help of orphans and widows in their distress and keep oneself untarnished by the world.

℣ My sacrifice is a contrite spirit.
℟ A humbled, contrite heart you will not spurn, O God.

CONCLUDING PRAYER

Bend our wills, Lord, so that by this Lenten observance
we may fit ourselves to celebrate the Easter festival;
and as we have all undertaken to subdue the body,
may we all be renewed in spirit.
Though Christ our Lord.

SATURDAYS OF LENT

Before Noon

Ant. This is the time of repentance for us to atone for our sins and seek salvation.

SCRIPTURE READING REV 3:19-20

I am the one who reproves and disciplines all those he loves: so repent in real earnest. Look, I am standing at the door, knocking. If one of you hears me calling and opens the door, I will come in to share his meal, side by side with him.

℣ A pure heart create for me, O God.
℟ Put a steadfast spirit within me.

Midday

Ant. As I live, says the Lord, I have no pleasure in the death of the wicked man, rather let him turn from his evil way and live.

SCRIPTURE READING IS 44:21-22

Remember that you are my servant; Israel, I have formed you, you are my servant, I will not forget you. I have dispelled your faults like a cloud, your sins like a mist. Come back to me, for I have redeemed you.

℣ From my sins turn away your face.
℟ And blot out all my guilt.

Afternoon

Ant. Armed with the justice which is the power of God, let us prove ourselves with great patience.

SCRIPTURE READING GAL 6:7b-8

Do not delude yourself into thinking God can be cheated: where a man sows, there he reaps; if he sows in the field of self-indulgence he will get a harvest of corruption out of it; if he sows in the field of the Spirit he will get from it a harvest of eternal life.
℣ My sacrifice is a contrite spirit.
℟ A humbled, contrite heart you will not spurn, O God.

CONCLUDING PRAYER

Turn our hearts to yourself, eternal Father,
so that, always seeking the one thing necessary
and devoting ourselves to works of charity,
we may worship you in spirit and in truth.
Through Christ our Lord.

HOLY WEEK

PALM SUNDAY OF THE PASSION OF THE LORD

Psalter: Week 2

Before Noon

Ant. Before the feast of the Passover Jesus knew that his hour had come. He had always loved those who were his, and now he showed the full extent of his love.

SCRIPTURE READING 2 COR 4:10-12

Wherever we go we carry death with us in our body, the death that Jesus died, that in this body also life may reveal itself, the life that Jesus lives. For continually, while still alive, we are being surrendered into the hands of death, for Jesus' sake, so that the life of Jesus also may be revealed in this mortal body of ours. Thus death is at work in us, and life in you.

℣ He was oppressed, and he was afflicted.

℟ Yet he opened not his mouth.

Midday

Ant. The Father knows me and I know the Father; and I lay down my life for my sheep.

SCRIPTURE READING 1 PET 4:13-14

If you can have some share in the sufferings of Christ, be glad, because you will enjoy a much greater gladness when his glory is revealed. It is a blessing for you when they insult you for bearing the name of Christ, because it means that you have the Spirit of glory, the Spirit of God resting on you.

℣ Ours were the sufferings he bore.

℟ Ours the sorrows he carried.

Afternoon

Ant. To me life is Christ, and death gain. I will glory in the cross of my Lord Jesus Christ.

SCRIPTURE READING 1 PET 5:10-11

You will have to suffer only for a little while: the God of all grace who called you to eternal glory in Christ will see that all is well again; he will confirm, strengthen, and support you. His power lasts for ever and ever. Amen.

℣ Let us venerate the sign of the cross.
℟ Through it we have received the sacrament of salvation.

CONCLUDING PRAYER

Almighty, ever-living God,
you gave our Saviour the command
to become man and undergo the cross,
as an example of humility for all men to follow.
We have the lessons of his sufferings:
give us also the fellowship of his resurrection.
Through Christ our Lord.

EASTER TRIDUUM

GOOD FRIDAY

PSALMODY

ANTIPHON
Before Noon: At the third hour Jesus was crucified.
Midday: From the sixth hour there was darkness over all the land until the ninth hour.
Afternoon: At the ninth hour, Jesus cried out in a loud voice, 'My God, my God, why have you deserted me?'

At one of these Hours the following psalms are said:

PSALM 39(40):2-14,17-18

I wáited, I wáited for the Lórd†
and he stóoped down to mé,*
he héard my crý.

He dréw me from the déadly pít,*
from the míry cláy.
He sét my féet upon a róck*
and made my fóotsteps fírm.

He pút a new sóng into my móuth,*
práise of our Gód.
Mány shall sée and féar*
and shall trúst in the Lórd.

Háppy the mán who has pláced*
his trúst in the Lórd
and has nót gone óver to the rébels*
who fóllow false góds.

How mány, O Lórd my Gód,†
(are the wónders and desígns
(that yóu have wórked for ús;*
you háve no équal.

Shóuld I procláim and spéak of them,*
they are móre than I can téll!

You do not ásk for sácrifice and ófferings,*
but an ópen éar.
You do not ásk for hólocaust and víctim.*
Instéad, here am Í.

In the scróll of the bóok it stands wrítten*
that Í should do your wíll.
My Gód, I delíght in your láw*
in the dépth of my héart.

Your jústice Í have procláimed*
in the gréat assémbly.
My líps I háve not séaled;*
you knów it, O Lórd.

I have not hídden your jústice in my héart*
but decláred your faithful hélp.
I have not hídden your lóve and your trúth*
from the gréat assémbly.

O Lórd, you wíll not withhóld*
your compássion from mé.
Your mérciful lóve and your trúth*
will álways guárd me.

For Í am besét with évils*
too mány to be cóunted.
My síns have fállen upón me*
and my síght fáils me.
They are móre than the háirs of my héad*
and my héart sínks.

O Lórd, cóme to my réscue,*
Lord, cóme to my áid.

O lét there be rejóicing and gládness*
for áll who séek you.
Let them éver say: 'The Lórd is gréat',*
who lóve your saving hélp.

As for mé, wrétched and póor,*
the Lórd thinks of mé.
Yóu are my réscuer, my hélp,*
O Gód, do not deláy.

PSALM 53(54):1-6,8-9

O Gód, sáve me by your náme;*
by your pówer, uphóld my cáuse.
O Gód, héar my práyer;*
listén to the wórds of my móuth.

For próud men have rísen agáinst me,†
rúthless men séek my lífe.*
They háve no regárd for Gód.
But Í have Gód for my hélp.*
The Lórd uphólds my lífe.

I will sácrifice to yóu with willing héart*
and práise your náme for it is góod:
for you have réscued me from áll my distréss*
and my éyes have seen the dównfall of my fóes.

PSALM 87(88)

Lord my Gód, I call for hélp by dáy;*
I crý at níght befóre you.
Let my práyer cóme into your présence.*
O túrn your éar to my crý.

For my sóul is fílled with évils;*
my lífe is on the brínk of the gráve.
I am réckoned as óne in the tómb:*
I have réached the énd of my stréngth,

like óne alóne among the déad;*
like the sláin lýing in their gráves;
like thóse you remémber no móre,*
cut óff, as they áre, from your hánd.

You have láid me in the dépths of the tómb,*
in pláces that are dárk, in the dépths.

Your ánger weighs dówn upón me:*
I am drówned benéath your wáves.

You have táken awáy my fríends*
and máde me háteful in their síght.
Imprísoned, I cánnot escápe;*
my éyes are súnken with grief.

I cáll to you, Lórd, all the day lóng;*
to yóu I strétch out my hánds.
Will you wórk your wónders for the déad?*
Will the shádes stánd and práise you?

Will your lóve be tóld in the gráve*
or your fáithfulness amóng the déad?
Will your wónders be knówn in the dárk*
or your jústice in the lánd of oblívion?

As for mé, Lord, I cáll to you for hélp:*
in the mórning my práyer comes befóre you.
Lórd, whý do you rejéct me?*
Whý do you híde your fáce?

Wrétched, close to déath from my yóuth,*
I have bórne your tríals; I am númb.
Your fúry has swépt down upón me;*
your térrors have útterly destróyed me.

They surróund me all the dáy like a flóod,*
they assáil me áll togéther.
Friend and néighbour you have táken away:*
my óne compánion is dárkness.

At the other Hours the complementary psalms, pp. 123 ff

Before Noon
Ant. At the third hour Jesus was crucified.

SCRIPTURE READING IS 53:2-3
Like a sapling he grew up in front of us, like a root in arid ground. Without beauty, without majesty we saw him, no looks to attract our

eyes; a thing despised and rejected by men, a man of sorrows and familiar with suffering, a man to make people screen their faces; he was despised and we took no account of him.
℣ We adore you, Christ, and we bless you,
℟ By your cross you have redeemed the world.

Midday

Ant. From the sixth hour there was darkness over all the land until the ninth hour.

SCRIPTURE READING IS 53:4-5

Ours were the sufferings he bore, ours the sorrows he carried. But we, we thought of him as someone punished, struck by God and brought low. He was pierced through for our faults, crushed for our sins. On him lies a punishment that brings us peace, and through his wounds we are healed.
℣ Lord, remember me,
℟ When you come into your kingdom.

Afternoon

Ant. At the ninth hour, Jesus cried out in a loud voice, 'My God, my God, why have you deserted me?'

SCRIPTURE READING IS 53:6-7

We had all gone astray like sheep, each taking his own way, and the Lord burdened him with the sins of all of us. Harshly dealt with, he bore it humbly, he never opened his mouth, like a lamb that is led to the slaughter-house, like a sheep that is dumb before its shearers never opening its mouth.
℣ He has made me dwell in darkness.
℟ Like the dead, long forgotten.

CONCLUDING PRAYER

Be mindful, Lord, of this your family,
for whose sake our Lord Jesus Christ, when betrayed,
did not hesitate to yield himself into his enemies' hands,
and undergo the agony of the cross:
Who lives and reigns for ever and ever.

EASTER SUNDAY
(and Low Sunday)

Hymn as in the psalter for Week 1 if only one Hour is said.

Psalms of Sunday, Week 1.

At the other Hours the complementary psalms, pp. 123 ff.

Before Noon

Ant. Christ has risen from the dead; he is no longer subject to death, alleluia.

SCRIPTURE READING Cf 1 COR 15:3b-5

Christ died for our sins, in accordance with the scriptures; he was buried; and he was raised to life on the third day, in accordance with the scriptures; he appeared first to Cephas and secondly to the Twelve.

℣ This is the day which was made by the Lord, alleluia.

℟ Let us rejoice and be glad, alleluia.

Midday

Ant. He was put to death for our sins and raised to life to justify us, alleluia.

SCRIPTURE READING EPH 2:4-6

God's mercy is so abundant, and his love for us is so great, that while we were spiritually dead in our disobedience he brought us to life with Christ; it is by God's grace that you have been saved. In our union with Christ Jesus he raised us up with him to rule with him in the heavenly world.

℣ This is the day which was made by the Lord, alleluia.

℟ Let us rejoice and be glad, alleluia.

Afternoon

Ant. Since you have been raised to life with Christ, you must look for the things of heaven, alleluia.

SCRIPTURE READING ROM 6:4

In our baptism, we have been buried with him, died like him, that so, just as Christ was raised up by his Father's power from the dead, we too might live and move in a new kind of existence.

℣ This is the day which was made by the Lord, alleluia.

℟ Let us rejoice and be glad, alleluia.

CONCLUDING PRAYER

Easter Sunday: On this day, Lord God,
you opened for us the way to eternal life
through your only Son's victory over death.
Grant that as we celebrate the feast of his resurrection
we may be renewed by your Holy Spirit
and rise again in the light of life.
Through Christ our Lord.

Low Sunday: God of eternal compassion,
each Easter you rekindle the faith of your consecrated people.
Give them still greater grace,
so that all may truly understand
the waters in which they were cleansed,
the Spirit by which they were reborn,
the blood by which they were redeemed.
Through Christ our Lord.

SUNDAYS OF THE EASTER SEASON

Sundays 3 and 7: Psalter Week 3
Sunday 4: Psalter Week 4
Sunday 5: Psalter Week 1
Sunday 6: Psalter Week 2

Before Noon

SCRIPTURE READING Cf 1 COR 15:3b-5

Christ died for our sins, in accordance with the scriptures; he was buried; and he was raised to life on the third day, in accordance with the scriptures; he appeared first to Cephas and secondly to the Twelve.

℣ The Lord has truly risen, alleluia.

℟ He has appeared to Simon, alleluia.

Midday

SCRIPTURE READING EPH 2:4-6

God's mercy is so abundant, and his love for us is so great, that while we were spiritually dead in our disobedience he brought us to life with Christ; it is by God's grace that you have been saved. In our union with Christ Jesus he raised us up with him to rule with him in the heavenly world.

℣ The disciples rejoiced, alleluia.
℟ When they saw the Lord, alleluia.

Afternoon

SCRIPTURE READING ROM 6:4

In our baptism, we have been buried with him, died like him, that so, just as Christ was raised up by his Father's power from the dead, we too might live and move in a new kind of existence.

℣ Stay with us, Lord, alleluia.
℟ Since evening is approaching, alleluia.

CONCLUDING PRAYER

Lord God,
grant your people constant joy
in the renewed vigour of their souls.
They rejoice because you have restored them
to the glory of your adopted children:
let them look forward gladly
in the certain hope of resurrection.
Through Christ our Lord.

MONDAYS OF THE EASTER SEASON

Weeks 2 and 6: Psalter Week 2
Week 3: Psalter Week 3
Week 4: Psalter Week 4
Week 5: Psalter Week 1

Before Noon

SCRIPTURE READING REV 1:17c-18

I saw the Son of Man and he said to me, I am before all, I am at the end of all, and I live. I, who underwent death am alive, as you see, to endless ages, and I hold the keys of death and hell.

℣ The Lord has truly risen, alleluia.
℟ He has appeared to Simon, alleluia.

Midday

SCRIPTURE READING COL 2:9,10a,12

The full content of divine nature lives in Christ, in his humanity, and you have been given full life in union with him. For when you were baptized, you were buried with Christ, and in baptism you were also raised with Christ through your faith in the active power of God who raised him from death.

℣ The disciples rejoiced, alleluia.
℟ When they saw the Lord, alleluia.

Afternoon

SCRIPTURE READING 2 TIM 2:8,11

Remember Jesus Christ, who was raised from death, who was a descendant of David, as told in the Good News I preach. This is a true saying: If we have died with him, we shall also live with him.

℣ Stay with us, Lord, alleluia.
℟ Since evening is approaching, alleluia.

CONCLUDING PRAYER

Almighty, ever-living God,
we confidently call you Father as well as Lord.
Renew your Spirit in our hearts,
make us ever more perfectly your children,

so that we may enter upon the inheritance you have promised us.
Through Christ our Lord.

TUESDAYS OF THE EASTER SEASON

Before Noon

SCRIPTURE READING Cf ACTS 4:11-12

Jesus is the one of whom the scripture says: The stone that you the builders despised turned out to be the most important stone. Salvation is to be found through him alone; for there is no one else in all the world, whose name God has given to men, by whom we can be saved.

℣ The Lord has truly risen, alleluia.
℟ He has appeared to Simon, alleluia.

Midday

SCRIPTURE READING Cf 1 PET 3:21-22a

Baptism now saves you, not by washing off bodily dirt, but by the promise made to God from a good conscience. Baptism saves you through the resurrection of Jesus Christ, who has gone to heaven and is at the right side of God.

℣ The disciples rejoiced, alleluia,
℟ When they saw the Lord, alleluia.

Afternoon

SCRIPTURE READING COL 3:1-2

You have been raised to life with Christ. Set your hearts, then, on the things that are in heaven, where Christ sits on his throne at the right side of God. Keep your minds fixed on things there, not on things here on earth.

℣ Stay with us, Lord, alleluia,
℟ Since evening is approaching, alleluia.

CONCLUDING PRAYER

Almighty God,
give your Church the grace
to proclaim the power of Jesus, our Risen Lord.
We have received the first fruits of his grace:

prepare us for the full revelation of his gifts.
Through Christ our Lord.

WEDNESDAYS OF THE EASTER SEASON

Before Noon

SCRIPTURE READING Cf ROM 4:24-25

We believe in him who raised Jesus our Lord from the dead, Jesus who was put to death for our sins and raised to life to justify us.

℣ The Lord has truly risen, alleluia.
℟ He has appeared to Simon, alleluia.

Midday

SCRIPTURE READING 1 JN 5:5-6a

Who can overcome the world? Only the man who believes that Jesus is the Son of God: Jesus Christ, who came by water and blood, not with water only, but with water and blood.

℣ The disciples rejoiced, alleluia.
℟ When they saw the Lord, alleluia.

Afternoon

SCRIPTURE READING EPH 4:23-24

You must put on the new self, which is created in God's likeness, and reveals itself in the true life that is upright and holy.

℣ Stay with us, Lord, alleluia.
℟ Since evening is approaching, alleluia.

CONCLUDING PRAYER

Year by year, Lord,
we recall the mystery of Easter,
the mystery which restored mankind to its lost dignity
and brought the hope of resurrection.
Grant that we may possess eternally in love
what we now worship in faith.
Through Christ our Lord.

THURSDAYS OF THE EASTER SEASON

Before Noon

SCRIPTURE READING 1 COR 12:13

We, too, all of us, have been baptized into a single body by the power of a single Spirit, Jews and Greeks, slaves and free men alike; we have all been given drink at a single source, the one Spirit.

℣ The Lord has truly risen, alleluia.
℟ He has appeared to Simon, alleluia.

Midday

SCRIPTURE READING TIT 3:5b-7

God saved us through the washing by which the Holy Spirit gives us new birth and new life. For God abundantly poured out the Holy Spirit on us, through Jesus Christ our Saviour, that by his grace we might be made right with God and come into possession of the eternal life we hope for.

℣ The disciples rejoiced, alleluia,
℟ When they saw the Lord, alleluia.

Afternoon

SCRIPTURE READING COL 1:12-14

Give thanks, with joy, to the Father who has made you fit to have your share of what God has reserved for his people in the kingdom of light. For he rescued us from the power of darkness and brought us safe into the kingdom of his dear Son, by whom we are set free and our sins are forgiven.

℣ Stay with us, Lord, alleluia.
℟ Since evening is approaching, alleluia.

CONCLUDING PRAYER

God of mercy,
let the mystery we celebrate at Eastertide
bear fruit for us in every season.
Through Christ our Lord.

FRIDAYS OF THE EASTER SEASON

Before Noon

SCRIPTURE READING ACTS 2:32,36

God has raised Jesus from the dead, and we are all witnesses to this fact. All the people of Israel, then, are to know for sure that it is this Jesus, whom you nailed to the cross, that God has made Lord and Messiah!

℣ The Lord has truly risen, alleluia.

℟ He has appeared to Simon, alleluia.

Midday

SCRIPTURE READING GAL 3:27-28

All you who have been baptized in Christ's name have put on the person of Christ; no more Jew or Gentile, no more slave and free man, no more male and female; you are all one person in Jesus Christ.

℣ The disciples rejoiced, alleluia.

℟ When they saw the Lord, alleluia.

Afternoon

SCRIPTURE READING 1 COR 5:7,8

You must take out this old yeast of sin so that you will be entirely pure. Then you will be like a new batch of dough without any yeast, as indeed I know you actually are. For our Passover feast is ready, now that Christ, our Passover lamb, has been sacrificed. Let us celebrate our feast, then, not with bread having the old yeast, the yeast of sin and immorality, but with the bread that has no yeast, the bread of purity and truth.

℣ Stay with us, Lord, alleluia,

℟ Since evening is approaching, alleluia.

CONCLUDING PRAYER

By your will, Lord God,
your Son underwent the agony of the cross
to break the power of Satan over man.
Give your people grace to rise again with Christ,
who lives and reigns for ever and ever.

SATURDAYS OF THE EASTER SEASON

Before Noon

SCRIPTURE READING ROM 5:10-11

Enemies of God, we were reconciled to him through his Son's death; reconciled to him, we are surer than ever of finding salvation in his Son's life. And, what is more, we can boast of God's protection, always through our Lord Jesus Christ, since it is through him that we have attained our reconciliation.

℣ The Lord has truly risen, alleluia.
℟ He has appeared to Simon, alleluia.

Midday

SCRIPTURE READING 1 COR 15:20-22

Christ has in fact been raised from the dead, the first fruits of all who have fallen asleep. Death came through one man and in the same way the resurrection of the dead has come through one man. Just as all men die in Adam, so all men will be brought to life in Christ.

℣ The disciples rejoiced, alleluia,
℟ When they saw the Lord, alleluia.

Afternoon

SCRIPTURE READING 2 COR 5:14-15

With us, Christ's love is a compelling motive, and this is the conviction we have reached: if one man died on behalf of all, then all thereby became dead men; Christ died for us all, so that being alive should no longer mean living with our own life, but with his life who died for us and has risen again.

℣ Stay with us, Lord, alleluia,
℟ Since evening is approaching, alleluia.

CONCLUDING PRAYER

Since it is from you, God our Father,
that redemption comes to us, your adopted children:
look with favour on the family you love,
give true freedom to us and to all who believe in Christ,
and bring us all alike to our eternal heritage.
Through Christ our Lord.

THE ASCENSION OF THE LORD

Solemnity

At one of these Hours the following psalms are said:

Ps 8, (Saturday Morning Prayer, Week 2), Ps 18A, (Monday Morning Prayer, Week 2), and Ps 18B, p 13.

At the other Hours the complementary psalms, pp. 123 ff.

Before Noon
Ant. Lord God, your majesty is praised above the heavens, alleluia.

SCRIPTURE READING REV 1:17c-18
I saw the Son of Man and he said to me, I am before all, I am at the end of all, and I live. I, who underwent death, am alive, as you see, to endless ages, and I hold the keys of death and hell.
℣ Do not let your hearts be troubled, alleluia.
℟ I am going to my Father, alleluia.

Midday
Ant. His rising is at one end of the heavens, and his course reaches their farthest ends, alleluia.

SCRIPTURE READING HEB 8:1b-3a
This high priest of ours is one who has taken his seat in heaven, on the right hand of that throne where God sits in majesty, ministering now in the sanctuary, in that true tabernacle which the Lord, not man, has set up. After all, it is the very function of a priest to offer gift and sacrifice.
℣ The Lord prepared a throne for him, alleluia.
℟ He established his kingdom in the heavens, alleluia.

Afternoon
Ant. He lifted up his hands and he blessed them. And as he blessed them he was taken up to heaven, alleluia.

SCRIPTURE READING COL 3:1-2
You have been raised to life with Christ. Set your hearts, then, on the things that are in heaven, where Christ sits on his throne at the right side

of God. Keep your minds fixed on things there, not on things here on earth.
℣ Give praise to the King of kings, alleluia.
℟ Sing a hymn to God, alleluia.

CONCLUDING PRAYER
Almighty God,
fill us with a holy joy,
teach us how to thank you with reverence and love
on account of the ascension of Christ your Son.
You have raised us up with him:
where he, the head, has preceded us in glory,
there we, the body, are called in hope.
Through Christ our Lord.

PENTECOST SUNDAY

Solemnity

At one of these Hours Ps 117, Sunday Week 1, pp. 10 ff, is said.

At the other Hours the complementary psalms.

Before Noon
Ant. The Holy Spirit came from the throne of God, and entered invisibly into the hearts of the apostles, alleluia.

SCRIPTURE READING 1 COR 12:13
We too, all of us, have been baptized into a single body by the power of a single Spirit, Jews and Greeks, slaves and free men alike; we have all been given drink at a single source, the one Spirit.
℣ The Holy Spirit is the Advocate, alleluia.
℟ He will teach you all things, alleluia.

Midday
Ant. Lord, grant us an increase of faith, and let the light of the Holy Spirit fill us always, alleluia.

SCRIPTURE READING TIT 3:5b-7

God saved us through the washing by which the Holy Spirit gives us new birth and new life. For God abundantly poured out the Holy Spirit on us through Jesus Christ our Saviour, that by his grace we might be made right with God and come into possession of the eternal life we hope for.
℣ The Holy Spirit will teach you, alleluia.
℟ Then you will understand all the things I have said, alleluia.

Afternoon

Ant. It is not you who will be speaking; the Spirit of your Father will be speaking in you, alleluia.

SCRIPTURE READING 2 COR 1:21-22

If you and we belong to Christ, guaranteed as his and anointed, it is all God's doing; it is God also who has set his seal upon us, and as a pledge of what is to come has given the Spirit to dwell in our hearts.
℣ The apostles spoke in different tongues, alleluia.
℟ They proclaimed the wonderful deeds of God, alleluia.

CONCLUDING PRAYER

Almighty God,
let the splendour of your glory shine upon us.
May Christ, who is light from your light,
strengthen, by the illumination of the Holy Spirit,
the hearts of those who have been reborn by grace.
Through Christ our Lord.

SOLEMNITIES OF THE LORD IN ORDINARY TIME

Sunday after Pentecost

THE MOST HOLY TRINITY

Solemnity

Psalms of Sunday, Week 1, pp. 9 ff.

Before Noon

Ant. We call upon you, we praise you, we worship you, O blessed Trinity.

SCRIPTURE READING 2 COR 1:21-22

If you and we belong to Christ, guaranteed as his and anointed, it is all God's doing; it is God who has set his seal upon us, and as a pledge of what is to come has given the Spirit to dwell in our hearts.

℣ Enter his doors with shouts of joy.

℟ Give glory to the Father and to the Son and to the Holy Spirit.

Midday

Ant. You are our hope, our salvation and our glory, O blessed Trinity.

SCRIPTURE READING GAL 4:4,5-6

God sent his Son to enable us to be adopted as sons. The proof that you are sons is that God has sent the Spirit of his Son into our hearts, the Spirit that cries 'Abba, Father'.

℣ We call upon you, O holy Trinity, blessed and glorious.

℟ Hear us, Father, Son and Holy Spirit.

Afternoon

Ant. We profess that it is always one and the same thing for you to be, to live, to know.

SCRIPTURE READING REV 7:12

Praise and glory and wisdom and thanks and honour and power and might belong to our God for ever and ever. Amen.

℣ Lord, you are blessed in the vault of heaven.
℟ You are exalted and glorified above all else for ever.

CONCLUDING PRAYER

God our Father,
you revealed the great mystery of your godhead to men
when you sent into the world
the Word who is Truth
and the Spirit who makes us holy.
Help us to believe in you and worship you,
as the true faith teaches:
three Persons, eternal in glory,
one God, infinite in majesty.
Through Christ our Lord.

Thursday after Holy Trinity
In Australia, Sunday after Trinity Sunday

THE BODY AND BLOOD OF CHRIST

Solemnity

Where the Solemnity of the Body and Blood of Christ is not a holyday of obligation, it is assigned to the Sunday following Holy Trinity as its proper day.

The complementary psalms, pp. 123 ff. Where the Solemnity is celebrated on a Sunday the psalms are of Sunday, Week 1, pp. 9 ff.

Before Noon

Ant. I have desired greatly to eat this Paschal supper with you before I suffer, alleluia.

SCRIPTURE READING WIS 16:20

And your own people Lord? Them you did foster with the food of angels; bread from heaven you set before them, which no labour of theirs had made ready, every taste uniting that could bring content, of every appetite the welcome choice.
℣ I will go to the altar of God, alleluia.
℟ I will partake of Christ who renews my youth, alleluia.

Midday

Ant. While they were at supper, Jesus took bread into his hands, he blessed it, broke it, and gave it to his disciples, alleluia.

SCRIPTURE READING PROV 9:1-2

Wisdom has built herself a house, she has erected her seven pillars, she has slaughtered her beasts, prepared her wine, she has laid her table.
℣ You have fed them with bread from heaven, alleluia.
℟ And that bread contained all goodness, alleluia.

Afternoon

Ant. They recognized the Lord Jesus by the breaking of the bread, alleluia.

SCRIPTURE READING ACTS 2:42,47

They met constantly to hear the apostles teach, and to share the common life, to break bread and to pray, as they praised God and enjoyed the favour of the whole people.
℣ Stay with us, Lord, alleluia.
℟ It is nearly evening and the day is drawing to a close, alleluia.

CONCLUDING PRAYER

Lord Jesus Christ,
you gave your Church an admirable sacrament
as the abiding memorial of your passion.
Teach us so to worship
the sacred mystery of your Body and Blood,
that its redeeming power
may sanctify us always.
Who live and reign for ever and ever.

Friday after the Second Sunday after Pentecost

THE MOST SACRED HEART OF JESUS

Solemnity

Complementary psalms pp. 123 ff.

Before Noon

Ant. My people, what have I done to you, how have I offended you? Answer me.

SCRIPTURE READING JER 31:2-4

The Lord says this: They have found pardon in the wilderness, those who have survived the sword. Israel is marching to his rest. The Lord has appeared to him from afar: I have loved you with an everlasting love, so I am constant in my affection for you. I build you once more; you shall be rebuilt.

℣ In joy you will draw water.

℟ You will drink from the spring of the Saviour.

Midday

Ant. My heart is stricken within me and all my bones tremble.

SCRIPTURE READING JER 32:40

I will make an everlasting covenant with them; I will not cease in my efforts for their good, and I will put respect for me into their hearts, so that they turn from me no more.

℣ I looked in vain for compassion.

℟ I sought consolation, but there was none to be found.

Afternoon

Ant. One of the soldiers opened the side of Jesus with his lance, and immediately there gushed forth blood and water.

SCRIPTURE READING ROM 5:8-9

Christ died for us while we were yet sinners, and that is God's own proof of his love towards us. And so, since we have now been justified by Christ's sacrificial death, we shall all the more certainly be saved through him from final retribution.

℣ He was wounded because of our sins.
℟ Through his wounds we are healed.

CONCLUDING PRAYER

Almighty God and Father,
we glory in the Sacred Heart of Jesus, your beloved Son,
as we call to mind the great things his love has done for us.
Fill us with the grace that flows in abundance
from the Heart of Jesus, the source of heaven's gifts.
Through Christ our Lord.

SUNDAYS IN ORDINARY TIME

WEEK 1

Psalter: Week 1

The Feast of the Baptism of the Lord takes the place of the Sunday.

SUNDAY 2

Psalter: Week 2

CONCLUDING PRAYER
Almighty God,
ruler of all things in heaven and on earth,
listen favourably to the prayer of your people,
and grant us your peace in our day.
Through Christ our Lord.

SUNDAY 3

Psalter: Week 3

CONCLUDING PRAYER
All-powerful, ever-living God,
direct our steps in the way of your love,
so that our whole life may be fragrant
with all we do in the name of Jesus, your beloved Son,
who lives and reigns for ever and ever.

SUNDAY 4

Psalter: Week 4

CONCLUDING PRAYER
Lord our God,
make us love you above all things,

and all our fellow-men
with a love that is worthy of you.
Through Christ our Lord.

SUNDAY 5

Psalter: Week 1

CONCLUDING PRAYER
Guard your family, Lord, with constant loving care,
for in your divine grace we place our only hope.
Through Christ our Lord.

SUNDAY 6

Psalter: Week 2

CONCLUDING PRAYER
To those who love you, Lord,
you promise to come with your Son
and make your home within them.
Come then with your purifying grace
and make our hearts a place where you can dwell.
Through Christ our Lord.

SUNDAY 7

Psalter: Week 3

CONCLUDING PRAYER
Grant, almighty God,
that with our thoughts always on the things of the Spirit
we may please you in all that we say and do.
Through Christ our Lord.

SUNDAY 8

Psalter: Week 4

CONCLUDING PRAYER
In your mercy, Lord, direct the affairs of men so peaceably
that your Church may serve you in tranquillity and joy.
Through Christ our Lord.

SUNDAY 9

Psalter: Week 1

CONCLUDING PRAYER
Lord God, by whom our lives are governed with unfailing wisdom and love,
take away from us all that is harmful
and give us all that will be for our good.
Through Christ our Lord.

SUNDAY 10

Psalter: Week 2

CONCLUDING PRAYER
Lord God, source of all good,
hear our prayer:
inspire us with good intentions,
and help us to fulfil them.
Through Christ our Lord.

SUNDAY 11

Psalter: Week 3

CONCLUDING PRAYER

Lord God, strength of those who hope in you,
support us in our prayer:
because we are weak and can do nothing without you,
give us always the help of your grace
so that, in fulfilling your commandments,
we may please you in all we desire to do.
Through Christ our Lord.

SUNDAY 12

Psalter: Week 4

CONCLUDING PRAYER

Lord God,
teach us at all times to fear and love your holy name,
for you never withdraw your guiding hand
from those you establish in your love.
Through Christ our Lord.

SUNDAY 13

Psalter: Week 1

CONCLUDING PRAYER

Lord God,
since by the adoption of grace,
you have made us children of light:
do not let false doctrine darken our minds,
but grant that your light may shine within us
and we may always live in the brightness of truth.
Through Christ our Lord.

SUNDAY 14

Psalter: Week 2

CONCLUDING PRAYER
Lord God,
when our world lay in ruins
you raised it up again
on the foundation of your Son's passion and death;
give us grace to rejoice in the freedom from sin
which he gained for us,
and bring us to everlasting joy.
Through Christ our Lord.

SUNDAY 15

Psalter: Week 3

CONCLUDING PRAYER
God and Father,
to those who go astray you reveal the light of your truth
and enable them to return to the right path:
grant that all who have received the grace of baptism
may strive to be worthy of their Christian calling,
and reject everything opposed to it.
Through Christ our Lord.

SUNDAY 16

Psalter: Week 4

CONCLUDING PRAYER
Be gracious, Lord, to us who serve you,
and in your kindness increase your gifts of grace within us:
so that fervent in faith, hope and love
we may be ever on the watch
and persevere in doing what you command.
Through Christ our Lord.

SUNDAY 17

Psalter: Week 1

CONCLUDING PRAYER

Lord God, protector of those who hope in you,
without whom nothing is strong, nothing holy,
support us always with your love.
Guide us so to use the good things of this world,
that even now we may hold fast to what endures for ever.
Through Christ our Lord.

SUNDAY 18

Psalter: Week 2

CONCLUDING PRAYER

We recognize with joy
that you, Lord, created us,
and that you guide us by your providence.
In your unfailing kindness
support us in our prayer:
renew your life within us,
guard it and make it bear fruit for eternity.
Through Christ our Lord.

SUNDAY 19

Psalter: Week 3

CONCLUDING PRAYER

Almighty, ever-living God,
we confidently call you Father as well as Lord.
Renew your Spirit in our hearts,
make us ever more perfectly your children,
so that we may enter upon the inheritance you have promised us.
Through Christ our Lord.

SUNDAY 20

Psalter: Week 4

CONCLUDING PRAYER

Lord God,
you have prepared for those who love you
what no eye has seen, no ear has heard.
Fill our hearts with your love,
so that loving you above all and in all,
we may attain your promises
which the heart of man has not conceived.
Through Christ our Lord.

SUNDAY 21

Psalter: Week 1

CONCLUDING PRAYER

Lord, by your grace we are made one in mind and heart.
Give us a love for what you command
and a longing for what you promise,
so that, amid this world's changes,
our hearts may be set on the world of lasting joy.
Through Christ our Lord.

SUNDAY 22

Psalter: Week 2

CONCLUDING PRAYER

Father of might and power,
every good and perfect gift
comes down to us from you.
Implant in our hearts the love of your name,
increase our zeal for your service,
nourish what is good in us
and tend it with watchful care.
Through Christ our Lord.

SUNDAY 23

Psalter: Week 3

CONCLUDING PRAYER

Since it is from you, God our Father,
that redemption comes to us, your adopted children:
look with favour on the family you love,
give true freedom to us and to all who believe in Christ,
and bring us all alike to our eternal heritage.
Through Christ our Lord.

SUNDAY 24

Psalter: Week 4

CONCLUDING PRAYER

Look upon us, Lord, creator and ruler of the whole world:
give us grace to serve you with all our heart
that we may come to know the power of your forgiveness and love.
Through Christ our Lord.

SUNDAY 25

Psalter: Week 1

CONCLUDING PRAYER

Father,
you summed up the whole law
as love of you and of our neighbour.
Grant that by keeping this commandment of love,
we may come to eternal life.
Through Christ our Lord.

SUNDAY 26

Psalter: Week 2

CONCLUDING PRAYER

Lord,
you reveal your mighty power
most of all by your forgiveness and compassion:
fill us constantly with your grace
as we hasten to share the joys you have promised us in heaven.
Through Christ our Lord.

SUNDAY 27

Psalter: Week 3

CONCLUDING PRAYER

Almighty, ever-living God,
whose love surpasses all that we ask or deserve,
open up for us the treasures of your mercy.
Forgive us all that weighs on our conscience,
and grant us more even than we dare to ask.
Through Christ our Lord.

SUNDAY 28

Psalter: Week 4

CONCLUDING PRAYER

Lord God,
open our hearts to your grace,
Let it go before us and be with us,
that we may always be intent upon doing your will.
Through Christ our Lord.

SUNDAY 29

Psalter: Week 1

CONCLUDING PRAYER

Almighty, ever-living God,
make us ever obey you willingly and promptly.
Teach us how to serve you
with sincere and upright hearts
in every sphere of life.
Through Christ our Lord.

SUNDAY 30

Psalter: Week 2

CONCLUDING PRAYER

Lord God, deepen our faith,
strengthen our hope,
enkindle our love:
and so that we may obtain what you promise
make us love what you command.
Through Christ our Lord.

SUNDAY 31

Psalter: Week 3

CONCLUDING PRAYER

God of power and mercy,
by whose grace your people give you praise and worthy service:
save us from faltering on our way
to the joys you have promised.
Through Christ our Lord.

SUNDAY 32

Psalter: Week 4

CONCLUDING PRAYER
Defend us, Lord, against every distress
so that unencumbered in body and soul,
we may devote ourselves to your service in freedom and joy.
Through Christ our Lord.

SUNDAY 33

Psalter: Week 1

CONCLUDING PRAYER
Lord our God,
give us grace to serve you always with joy,
because our full and lasting happiness
is to make of our lives
a constant service to the Author of all that is good.
Through Christ our Lord.

Last Sunday of the Year
CHRIST THE KING

CONCLUDING PRAYER
Almighty, ever-living God,
it is your will
to unite the entire universe
under your beloved Son,
Jesus Christ, the King of heaven and earth.
Grant freedom to the whole of creation,
and let it praise and serve your majesty for ever.
Through Christ our Lord.

SAINTS OF THE GENERAL CALENDAR

SOLEMNITIES AND FEASTS

2 February

THE PRESENTATION OF THE LORD

Feast

Psalms and antiphons of the occurring weekday or Sunday.

Before Noon

SCRIPTURE READING IS 8:14

The Lord will become a sanctuary, and a stone of offence, and a rock of stumbling to both houses of Israel, a trap and a snare to the inhabitants of Jerusalem.

℣ The Lord has remembered his truth and his love.
℟ He is mindful of his love for the house of Israel.

Midday

SCRIPTURE READING IS 42:13

The Lord advances like a hero, his fury is stirred like a warrior's. He gives the war shout, raises the hue and cry, marches valiantly against his foes.

℣ All the ends of the earth have seen the salvation of our God.
℟ Shout to the Lord with joy all the earth.

Afternoon

SCRIPTURE READING IS 12:5-6

Sing in honour of the great deeds the Lord has done, make them known for all the world to hear. Cry aloud in praise, people of Sion; great is the Holy One of Israel, that dwells among you.

℣ Mercy and faithfulness have met.
℟ Justice and peace have embraced.

CONCLUDING PRAYER

Almighty, ever-living God,
on this day your Only-begotten Son

was presented in the temple,
in flesh and blood like ours:
purify us in mind and heart
that we may meet you in your glory.
Through Christ our Lord.

19 March

SAINT JOSEPH
Husband of the Blessed Virgin Mary

Solemnity

Complementary psalms, pp. 123 ff.

Before Noon

Ant. Every year the parents of Jesus used to go to Jerusalem for the feast of the Passover (alleluia).

SCRIPTURE READING PROV 2:7-8

The Lord stores up sound wisdom for the upright; he is a shield to those who walk in integrity, guarding the paths of justice, and preserving the way of his saints.

℣ He made him master of his house (alleluia).
℟ He constituted him ruler of all he possessed (alleluia).

Midday

Ant. When they were on their way home after the feast the boy Jesus stayed behind in Jerusalem without his parents knowing it.

SCRIPTURE READING WIS 10:10

When her faithful servant was in flight, Wisdom guided him straight to his goal, and on the way showed him the heavenly kingdom, gave him knowledge of holy things. She enriched him by his toil, and gave all his labours a happy issue.

℣ Riches and wealth are in his house (alleluia).
℟ His justice stands firm for ever (alleluia).

Afternoon

Ant. When they could not find Jesus, his parents returned to Jerusalem and looked for him there.

SCRIPTURE READING SIR 2:18-19

Those who fear the Lord will not disobey his words, and those who love him will keep his ways. Those who fear the Lord will seek his approval, and those who love him will be filled with the law.

℣ Your saving help has given him glory (alleluia).

℟ You have laid upon him majesty and splendour (alleluia).

CONCLUDING PRAYER

Almighty God,
at the beginnings of our salvation,
when Mary conceived your Son and brought him forth into the world,
you placed them under Joseph's watchful care.
May his prayer still help your Church
to be an equally faithful guardian of your mysteries,
and a sign of Christ to mankind.
Through Christ our Lord.

25 March

THE ANNUNCIATION OF THE LORD

Solemnity

Complementary psalms, pp. 123 ff.

Before Noon

Ant. The virgin Mary was of the stock of Jesse; the Spirit of the Most High came to dwell within her (alleluia).

SCRIPTURE READING EPH 1:9b-10

Such was God's will and pleasure determined beforehand in Christ to be put into effect when the time was ripe: namely that the universe, all in heaven and on earth, might be brought into a unity in Christ.

℣ The angel of the Lord brought the good news to Mary (alleluia).

℟ And she conceived by the power of the Holy Spirit (alleluia).

Midday

Ant. Behold the virgin will conceive and bear a son, and his name will be called Immanuel (alleluia).

SCRIPTURE READING 1 JN 4:10

This is what love is: it is not that we have loved God, but that he loved us and sent his Son to be the means by which our sins are forgiven.
℣ I am the servant of the Lord (alleluia).
℟ Let it be done to me as you have said (alleluia).

Afternoon

Ant. He will extend his power to the ends of the earth: he himself will be our peace (alleluia).

SCRIPTURE READING 1 TIM 2:5

There is one God, and there is one who brings God and men together, the man Christ Jesus, who gave himself to redeem all men.
℣ The Word was made flesh (alleluia).
℟ He dwelt amongst us (alleluia).

CONCLUDING PRAYER

Shape us in the likeness of the divine nature of our Redeemer,
whom we believe to be true God and true man,
since it was your will, Lord God,
that he, your Word,
should take to himself our human nature
in the womb of the Blessed Virgin Mary.
Through Christ our Lord.

24 June

THE BIRTHDAY OF SAINT JOHN THE BAPTIST

Solemnity

Complementary psalms, pp. 123 ff. On a Sunday, the psalms of Sunday, Week 1, pp. 9 ff.

Before Noon

Ant. He will be great in the sight of God; he will be filled with the Holy Spirit from his mother's womb.

SCRIPTURE READING IS 49:1

Islands, listen to me, pay attention, remotest peoples. The Lord called me before I was born; from my mother's womb he pronounced my name.

℣ I saw the Holy Spirit descending and resting on him.

℟ He is the one who will baptize you in the Holy Spirit.

Midday

Ant. When I heard your greeting, the child in my womb leaped for joy, alleluia.

SCRIPTURE READING IS 49:5-6

And now the Lord has spoken, he who formed me in the womb to be his servant: 'I will make you the light of the nations so that my salvation may reach to the ends of the earth.'

℣ The Lord called me before I was born.

℟ From my mother's womb he pronounced my name.

Afternoon

Ant. This child will be great in the sight of the Lord, for his hand is with him.

SCRIPTURE READING IS 49:7b

Kings will stand up when they see you, and princes will bow, for the sake of the Lord who has been faithful, the Holy One of Israel who has chosen you.

℣ I am putting my words into your mouth.
℟ I am setting you over peoples and kingdoms.

CONCLUDING PRAYER
Almighty God and Father,
you sent Saint John the Baptist to the people of Israel
to make them ready for Christ the Lord.
Give us the grace of joy in the Spirit,
and guide the hearts of all the faithful
in the way of salvation and peace.
Through Christ our Lord.

29 June
In Australia, the Sunday on or after 29 June

SAINTS PETER AND PAUL

Apostles

Solemnity

Complementary psalms, pp. 123 ff. On a Sunday, the psalms of Sunday, Week 1, pp. 9 ff.

Before Noon

Ant. While Peter was still speaking, the Holy Spirit came upon all those who were listening to him and they spoke in tongues and gave praise to God.

SCRIPTURE READING ACTS 15:7-9
God chose me from among you to preach the message of Good News to the Gentiles, so that they could hear and believe. And God, who knows the hearts of men, showed his approval of the Gentiles by giving the Holy Spirit to them, just as he had to us. He made no difference between us and them; he forgave them their sins because they believed.
℣ Their voice has gone out through all the earth.
℟ Their message to the ends of the world.

Midday

Ant. Peter went to the housetop to pray at about the sixth hour.

SCRIPTURE READING GAL 1:15-16a,17b-18a

He who had set me apart from the day of my birth and called me by his grace, saw fit to make his Son known in me, so that I could preach his gospel among the Gentiles. I went off into Arabia, and when I came back it was to Damascus; then when three years had passed, I did go up to Jerusalem.

℣ They observed the precepts of God.
℟ They kept his decrees.

Afternoon

Ant. Peter and John went up to the temple for prayer at the ninth hour.

SCRIPTURE READING 2 COR 4:13

Scripture says: 'I spoke because I believed.' In the same spirit of faith, we also speak because we believe. For we know that God who raised the Lord Jesus to life will also raise us up with Jesus and bring us together with you into his presence.

℣ Rejoice and be glad, said the Lord.
℟ Because your names are written in heaven.

CONCLUDING PRAYER

Almighty, ever-living God,
you give us the great joy of devoting this day
to the honour of the apostles Peter and Paul.
Grant that your Church
may follow their teaching to the full,
because these are the men
who first taught us to worship you in Christ, your Son,
who lives and reigns for ever and ever.

6 August

THE TRANSFIGURATION OF THE LORD

Feast

Psalms of the occurring weekday. Complementary psalms from Series II and III, pp. 126 ff, at the other Hours.

Before Noon

Ant. Jesus was transfigured between Moses and Elijah so that the Law and the Prophets might bear witness to him.

SCRIPTURE READING EX 19:9

The Lord said to Moses: 'Lo, I am coming to you in a thick cloud, that the people may hear when I speak with you, and may also believe you for ever.'

℣ You are the fairest of the children of men.

℟ Graciousness is poured upon your lips.

Midday

Ant. The Lord God our Saviour has proclaimed life and immortality through his gospel.

SCRIPTURE READING EX 33:9-11

When Moses entered the tent, the pillar of cloud would descend and stand at the door of the tent, and the Lord would speak with Moses. Thus the Lord used to speak to Moses face to face, as a man speaks to his friend.

℣ Look towards him and shine with joy.

℟ No longer hang your heads in shame.

Afternoon

Ant. When the disciples heard the voice of the Father they fell on their faces, overcome with fear.

SCRIPTURE READING 2 COR 3:18

All of us, then, reflect the glory of the Lord with uncovered faces; and that same glory, coming from the Lord who is the Spirit, transforms us into his very likeness, in an ever greater degree of glory.

℣ Lord, you are the source of life.
℟ In your light we see light.

CONCLUDING PRAYER

Father,
at the Transfiguration in glory of your Only-begotten Son,
you confirmed the mysteries of faith
by the witness to Jesus
of the prophets Moses and Elijah.
You foreshadowed there what we shall be
when you bring our sonship to its perfection.
Grant that by listening to the voice of Jesus
we may become heirs with him,
who lives and reigns for ever and ever.

15 August

THE ASSUMPTION OF THE BLESSED VIRGIN MARY

Solemnity

The Complementary psalms, pp. 123 ff. On a Sunday the psalms are of Sunday, Week 1, pp. 9 ff.
Ps 121 may be replaced by Ps 128, p. 112, and Ps 126 by Ps 130 (Tuesday Evening Prayer, Week 3).

Before Noon

Ant. You have been raised up like the cedar of Lebanon, like the cypress tree on Mount Sion, O holy Mother of God.

SCRIPTURE READING JUD 13:22,23b

The Lord has blessed you by his power, because by you he has brought our enemies to nought. Blessed are you, daughter, by the Lord the Most High God, above all women upon the earth.
℣ Mary has been assumed into heaven, the angels rejoice.
℟ They sing for joy and praise the Lord.

Midday

Ant. We acknowledge you as the Queen of Heaven, O Mary, for the Sun of Justice has come forth from your tent.

SCRIPTURE READING REV 12:1

A great sign appeared in heaven: a woman adorned with the sun, standing on the moon, and with twelve stars on her head for a crown.

℣ The Holy Mother of God is exalted for ever.

℟ She has been raised up above the choirs of angels to the kingdom of heaven.

Afternoon

Ant. The Holy Mother of God has been raised above the choirs of angels and has entered the kingdom of heaven.

SCRIPTURE READING 2 COR 5:1

We know that when this tent we live in — our body here on earth — is torn down, God will have a house in heaven for us to live in, a home he himself made, which will last for ever.

℣ The Virgin Mary has been assumed to the heavenly dwelling place.

℟ There the King of kings sits on a throne of stars.

CONCLUDING PRAYER

Almighty, ever-living God,
you have taken the mother of your Son,
the immaculate Virgin Mary,
body and soul into the glory where you dwell.
Keep our hearts set on heaven
so that, with her, we may share in your glory.
Through Christ our Lord.

14 September

THE EXALTATION OF THE HOLY CROSS

Feast

Psalms of the occurring Sunday or weekday.

Before Noon

Ant. Save us, Christ our Saviour, by the power of the cross. You saved Peter from the waves, have mercy on us.

SCRIPTURE READING HEB 5:7-9

During his life on earth, Christ offered up prayer and entreaty, aloud and in silent tears, to the one who had the power to save him out of death, and he submitted so humbly that his prayer was heard. Although he was Son, he learnt to obey through suffering, but having been made perfect, he became for all who obey him the source of eternal salvation.

℣ We worship you, Christ, and we bless you.

℟ By your cross you have redeemed the world.

Midday

Ant. Save us, Saviour of the world. By the cross and the shedding of your blood you have redeemed us. Come to help us, Lord, our God.

SCRIPTURE READING EPH 1:7-8

In Christ our release is secured and our sins are forgiven through the shedding of his blood. Therein lies the richness of God's free grace lavished upon us, imparting full wisdom and insight.

℣ Before you all the earth shall bow.

℟ All peoples shall sing to you, sing to your name.

Afternoon

Ant. Dying you destroyed our death, rising you restored our life.Save us by your cross, Christ our Redeemer.

SCRIPTURE READING 1 PET 1:18-19

Remember, the ransom that was paid to free you from the useless way of life your ancestors handed down was not paid in anything corruptible, neither in silver nor gold, but in the precious blood of a

lamb without stain, namely Christ.
℣ This sign of the cross will appear in the heavens.
℟ When the Lord will come as judge.

CONCLUDING PRAYER

God our Father,
in obedience to your will
your Only-begotten Son endured the cross for our salvation.
Grant that as we have come to know the mystery of the cross here on earth,
we may receive its rewards in heaven.
Through Christ our Lord.

1 November

ALL SAINTS

Solemnity

Complementary psalms, pp. 123 ff. On a Sunday, the psalms of Sunday, Week 1, pp. 9 ff.

Before Noon

Ant. The Lord will comfort Sion. Joy and gladness shall be found in her, thanksgiving and melody.

SCRIPTURE READING IS 65:18-19

Be glad and rejoice for ever and ever for what I am creating, because I now create Jerusalem, 'Joy' and her people 'Gladness'. I shall rejoice over Jerusalem and exult in my people. No more will the sound of weeping or the sound of cries be heard in her.
℣ Be glad and rejoice, all you saints.
℟ For your reward is great in heaven.

Midday

Ant. Nations will recount their wisdom, and God's people will sing their praises.

SCRIPTURE READING 1 PET 1:15-16

Be holy in all you do, since it is the Holy One who has called you, and scripture says, 'Be holy, for I am holy.'

℣ Sing psalms to the Lord, you who love him.
℟ Give thanks to his holy name.

Afternoon

Ant. The saints through faith conquered kingdoms, did what is right and earned the promises.

SCRIPTURE READING REV 21:10-11;22:3b-4

The Spirit took control of me, and the angel carried me to the top of a very high mountain. He showed me Jerusalem, the Holy City, coming down out of heaven from God, shining with the glory of God. The throne of God and of the Lamb will be in the city, and his servants will worship him. They will see his face, and his name will be written on their foreheads.

℣ The just will praise your name, Lord.
℟ The upright shall live in your presence.

CONCLUDING PRAYER

Almighty, ever-living God
we are celebrating with joy
the triumph of your grace in all the saints.
With so vast a multitude praying for us,
may we receive from you
the fulness of mercy we have always desired.
Through Christ our Lord.

2 November

ALL SOULS DAY

When 2 November is a Sunday, even though Mass may be of the Commemoration of All Souls, the Office celebrated is that of the Sunday, and the Office for the Dead is omitted.

From the Office for the Dead, pp. 213 ff.

9 November

DEDICATION OF THE LATERAN BASILICA

Feast

Psalms and antiphons of the day.

Before Noon

When the complementary psalms are used, Ps 121 may be replaced by Ps 128, p. 112.

SCRIPTURE READING 1 COR 3:16-17

Surely you know that you are God's temple, and that God's Spirit lives in you! So if anyone destroys God's temple, God will destroy him. For God's temple is holy, and you yourselves are his temple.

℣ Lord, I love the beauty of your house (alleluia).
℟ The place where your glory dwells (alleluia).

Midday

SCRIPTURE READING 2 COR 6:16

The temple of the living God is what we are. God's own words are: I will live and move about among them; I will be their God and they shall be my people.

℣ Pray for the peace of Jerusalem (alleluia).
℟ May those who love you prosper (alleluia).

Afternoon

SCRIPTURE READING JER 7:2b,4-5a,7a

Listen to the word of the Lord you who come in by these gates to worship the Lord. Put no trust in delusive words like these: 'This is the sanctuary of the Lord, the sanctuary of the Lord, the sanctuary of the Lord!' But if you do amend your behaviour and your actions, then here in this place I will stay with you.

℣ Enter the gates of the Lord with thanksgiving (alleluia).
℟ Walk into his courts with praise (alleluia).

CONCLUDING PRAYER

In the dedicated church only

Almighty God,
as we recall with joy
the dedication of this house of yours
on each recurring anniversary:
listen to your people's prayer,
and grant that our worship here
may be a sincere and holy service,
honouring your name
and bringing us the fulness of redemption.
Through Christ our Lord.

Outside the dedicated church itself

Lord God,
you choose men as living stones to become an eternal dwelling,
built to the glory of your name.
Increase your gifts of grace to the Church,
and let your your faithful people throng in ever greater numbers
to form the heavenly Jerusalem.
Through Christ our Lord.

Alternative

Lord God,
you have called your people to become your Church,
grant that all who are gathered in your name
may fear you and love you,
may follow you and, under your guidance,
attain to your promises in heaven.
Through Christ our Lord.

8 December

THE IMMACULATE CONCEPTION OF THE BLESSED VIRGIN MARY

Solemnity

The complementary psalms are used. Ps 121 may be replaced by Ps 128, p. 112, and Ps 126 by Ps 130 (Tuesday Evening Prayer, Week 3).

Before Noon

Ant. Praise God, who has not withdrawn his mercy from me.

SCRIPTURE READING EPH 1:4

Before the world was made, he chose us in Christ to be holy and spotless, and to live through love in his presence.

℣ Today we celebrate the Immaculate Conception of the Blessed Virgin Mary,

℟ Who crushed the head of the serpent with her foot.

Midday

Ant. The Lord will find his delight in you; your God will rejoice over you.

SCRIPTURE READING EPH 1:11-12a

It is in Christ that we were claimed as God's own, chosen from the beginning, under the predestined plan of the one who guides all things, as he decides by his own will, chosen for his greater glory.

℣ My heart and my flesh ring out their joy,

℟ To God, the living God.

Afternoon

Ant. God created me according to his truth; he took me by the hand and kept me safe from harm.

SCRIPTURE READING EPH 5:25-27

Christ loved the Church and sacrificed himself for her to make her holy, so that when he took her to himself she would be glorious, with no speck or wrinkle or anything like that, but holy and faultless.

℣ Your Immaculate Conception, O Virgin Mother of God,
℟ Brings joy to the whole world.

CONCLUDING PRAYER
Father,
we rejoice in the privilege of our Lady's Immaculate Conception,
which preserved her from the stain of sin
by the power of Christ's redeeming death,
and prepared her to be the Mother of God.
Grant that through her prayers
we ourselves may come to you,
cleansed from all sin.
Through Christ our Lord.

THE OFFICE FOR THE DEAD

The concluding prayers are to be changed in gender and number according to circumstances.
In Eastertide, 'Alleluia' may be added, if judged fitting, to the end of antiphons, versicles and responsories.

Hymn, from the appendix.

PSALMODY

ANTIPHON
Before Noon: Return, Lord, and rescue my soul.
Midday: Lord, heal my soul for I have sinned against you.
Afternoon: O God, save me by your name; by your power, uphold my cause.

PSALM 69(70)

O Gód, make háste to my réscue,*
Lord, cóme to my áid!
Lét there be sháme and confúsion*
on thóse who seek my lífe.

O lét them turn báck in confúsion,*
who delíght in my hárm,
let them retréat, cóvered with sháme,*
who jéer at my lót.

Lét there be rejóicing and gládness*
for áll who séek you.
Let them sáy for ever: 'Gód is gréat,'*
who lóve your saving hélp.

As for mé, wrétched and póor,*
cóme to me, O Gód.
Yóu are my réscuer, my hélp,*
O Lórd, do not deláy.

PSALM 84(85)

O Lórd, you once fávoured your lánd*
and revíved the fórtunes of Jácob,
you forgáve the guílt of your péople*
and cóvered áll their síns.
You avérted áll your ráge,*
you cálmed the héat of your ánger.

Revíve us now, Gód, our hélper!*
Put an énd to your gríevance agáinst us.
Will you be ángry with ús for éver,*
will your ánger néver céase?

Will you nót restóre again our lífe*
that your péople may rejóice in yóu?
Let us sée, O Lórd, your mércy*
and gíve us your sáving hélp.

I will héar what the Lord Gód has to sáy,*
a vóice that spéaks of péace,
péace for his péople and his fríends*
and those who túrn to hím in their héarts.
His help is néar for thóse who féar him*
and his glóry will dwéll in our lánd.

Mércy and faíthfulness have mét;*
jústice and péace have embráced.
Fáithfulness shall spríng from the éarth*
and jústice look dówn from héaven.

The Lórd will máke us prósper*
and our éarth shall yíeld its frúit.
Jústice shall márch befóre him*
and péace shall fóllow his stéps.

PSALM 85(86)

Turn your éar, O Lórd, and give ánswer*
for I am póor and néedy.
Preserve my lífe, for Í am fáithful:*
save the sérvant who trústs in yóu.

You are my Gód, have mércy on me, Lórd,*
for I crý to you áll the day lóng.
Give jóy to your sérvant, O Lórd,*
for to yóu I líft up my sóul.

O Lórd, you are góod and forgíving,*
full of lóve to áll who cáll.
Give héed, O Lórd, to my práyer*
and atténd to the sóund of my vóice.

In the dáy of distréss I will cáll*
and súrely yóu will replý.
Among the góds there is nóne like you, O Lórd;*
nor wórk to compáre with yóurs.

All the nátions shall cóme to adóre you*
and glórify your náme, O Lórd:
for you are gréat and do márvellous déeds,*
yóu who alóne are Gód.

Shów me, Lórd, your wáy†
so that Í may wálk in your trúth.*
Guide my héart to féar your náme.

I will práise you, Lord my Gód, with all my héart*
and glórify your náme for éver;

for your lóve to mé has been gréat:*
you have sáved me from the dépths of the gráve.

The próud have rísen agáinst me;†
rúthless men séek my lífe:*
to yóu they páy no héed.

But yóu, God of mércy and compássion,*
slów to ánger, O Lórd,
abóunding in lóve and trúth,*
túrn and take píty on mé.

O gíve your stréngth to your sérvant*
and sáve your hándmaid's són.
Shów me a sígn of your fávour†
that my fóes may sée to their sháme*
that you consóle me and gíve me your hélp.

At the other Hours the complementary psalms are taken from Series II and III, pp. 126 ff.

Before Noon

Ant. Return, Lord, and rescue my soul.

SCRIPTURE READING JOB 19:25-26

This I know: that my Redeemer lives, and he, the Last, will take his stand on earth. After my awaking, he will set me close to him, and from my flesh I shall look on God.

℣ Why are you cast down, my soul, why groan within me?

℟ Hope in God; I will praise him still.

Midday

Ant. Lord, heal my soul for I have sinned against you.

SCRIPTURE READING WIS 1:13-14a,15

Death was never of God's fashioning; not for his pleasure does life cease to be; what meant his creation, but that all created things should have being? No end nor term is fixed to a life well lived.

℣ In the midst of darkness and of death I will fear no evil.

℟ For you, Lord, are with me.

Afternoon

Ant. O God, save me by your name; by your power, uphold my cause.

SCRIPTURE READING IS 25:8

Death too shall be engulfed forever. No furrowed cheek but the Lord God will wipe away its tears; gone the contempt his people endured in a whole world's eyes; the Lord has promised it.

℣ O God, hear my prayer.
℟ To you all flesh will come.

CONCLUDING PRAYER

Grant, Lord, we pray,
that as our faith is built on the Risen Christ,
so too may our hope be steadfast,
as we await the resurrection of your servant N. from the dead.
Through Christ our Lord.

Alternative

For a Man

God, our Father,
by whose Son's death and resurrection we have been redeemed,
you are the glory of your faithful, the life of your saints:
have mercy on your servant N.,
and as he professed his faith in the mystery of our resurrection,
so may he gain possession of eternal joy.
Through Christ our Lord.

For a Woman

God, our Father,
by whose Son's death and resurrection we have been redeemed,
you are the glory of your faithful, the life of your saints:
have mercy on your servant N.,
and as she professed her faith in the mystery of our resurrection,
so may she gain possession of eternal joy.
Through Christ our Lord.

Alternative: In Ordinary Time

For a Man

Let our prayer come into your presence, Lord,
as we humbly ask for mercy:
and as in your love
you counted your servant N. among your people in this world,
so bring him now to the abode of peace and light,
and number him among your saints.
Through Christ our Lord.

For a Woman

Let our prayer come into your presence, Lord,
as we humbly ask for mercy:
and as in your love
you counted your handmaid N. among your people in this world,
so bring her now to the abode of peace and light,
and number her among your saints.
Through Christ our Lord.

Eastertide

God of mercy and power,
whose Son of his own free will
underwent a human death on our behalf:
let your servant N.
share in the admirable victory of Christ's resurrection.
Through Christ our Lord.

For several deceased

Lord God,
who gave your only-begotten Son
his place on high as conqueror of death:
grant to your servants N. and N. who have died,
that they in their turn may triumph over death,
and may live forever before you, their creator and redeemer.
Through Christ our Lord.

For Brethren, Relatives and Benefactors

Lord God,
as you are the fount of mercy and wish all men to be saved:
have mercy then on our deceased brethren, relatives and benefactors.

Through the intercession of Blessed Mary ever-virgin,
and of all your saints,
bring them to the fellowship of eternal joy.
Through Christ our Lord.

MEMORIA OF THE BLESSED VIRGIN MARY ON SATURDAY

On ordinary Saturdays Through the Year on which optional Memorias are allowed, an optional Memoria of the Blessed Virgin Mary may be celebrated.

All as in the psalter for the current Saturday.

APPENDIX

HYMNS FOR PRAYER DURING THE DAY

The following hymns are used at Prayer During the Day throughout the entire year. They are printed in the psalter, one to each week, but are here set out for the benefit of those who say more than one Hour of Prayer During the Day daily.
After each of the hymns for 'Before Noon', 'Midday' and 'Afternoon' the seasonal antiphons for the times are given, so that the sequence of use may be hymn, psalter, proper.

BEFORE NOON

HYMN

Come, Holy Spirit, live in us
With God the Father and the Son,
And grant us your abundant grace
To sanctify and make us one.

May mind and tongue made strong in love,
Your praise throughout the world proclaim,
And may that love within our hearts
Set fire to others with its flame.

Most blessed Trinity of love
For whom the heart of man was made,
To you be praise in timeless song,
And everlasting homage paid.

Stanbrook Abbey Hymnal

ANTIPHON

Advent: The prophets foretold that the Saviour would be born of the Virgin Mary.
Christmastide I (Before Epiphany): Joseph and Mary, the mother of Jesus, wondered at what was being said about him.
Christmastide II (After Epiphany): The mystery, which was hidden from earlier ages and generations, is now made clear.

Lent: This is the time of repentance for us to atone for our sins and seek salvation.
Holy Week (Monday to Thursday): Before the feast of the Passover Jesus knew that his hour had come. He had always loved those who were his, and now he showed the full extent of his love.
Easter Week: Christ has risen from the dead; he is no longer subject to death, alleluia.
Eastertide: Alleluia, alleluia, alleluia.

MIDDAY

HYMN

Lord God and Maker of all things,
Creation is upheld by you.
While all must change and know decay,
You are unchanging, always new.

You are man's solace and his shield,
His Rock secure on which to build;
You are the spirit's tranquil home,
In you alone is hope fulfilled.

To God the Father and the Son
And Holy Spirit render praise,
Blest Trinity, from age to age
The strength of all our living days.

Stanbrook Abbey Hymnal

ANTIPHON

Advent: The angel Gabriel said to Mary, 'Rejoice, most highly favoured one! The Lord is with you. Of all women you are the most blessed.'
Christmastide I (Before Epiphany): Mary treasured all these things and pondered them in her heart.
Christmastide II (After Epiphany): Christ came and preached peace to you who were far off, and peace to you who were near.
Lent: As I live, says the Lord, I have no pleasure in the death of the wicked man, rather let him turn from his evil way and live.
Holy Week (Monday to Thursday): The Father knows me and I know the Father; and I lay down my life for my sheep.

Easter Week: He was put to death for our sins and raised to life to justify us, alleluia.
Eastertide: Alleluia, alleluia, alleluia.

AFTERNOON

HYMN

Eternal Father, loving God,
Who made us from the dust of earth,
Transform us by the Spirit's grace,
Give value to our little worth.

Prepare us for that day of days
When Christ from heaven will come with might
To call us out of dust again,
Our bodies glorified in light.

O Godhead, here untouched, unseen,
All things created bear your trace;
The seed of glory sown in man
Will flower when we see your face.

Stanbrook Abbey Hymnal

ANTIPHON

Advent: Mary was greatly troubled at this greeting and wondered what it might mean. She said 'I am to give birth to a King without ceasing to be a virgin.'
Christmastide I (Before Epiphany): My eyes have seen the salvation which you prepared in the presence of all the peoples.
Christmastide II (After Epiphany): I have appointed you to be a light to all peoples, to be my saving power to the very ends of the earth.
Lent: Armed with the justice which is the power of God, let us prove ourselves with great patience.
Holy Week (Monday to Thursday): To me life is Christ, and death gain. I will glory in the cross of my Lord Jesus Christ.
Easter Week: Since you have been raised to life with Christ, you must look for the things of heaven, alleluia.
Eastertide: Alleluia, Alleluia, Alleluia.

FREQUENTLY RECURRING TEXTS

℣ O God, come to our aid.
℟ O Lord, make haste to help us.
Glory be to the Father and to the Son and to the Holy Spirit, as it was in the beginning, is now, and ever shall be, world without end. Amen. Alleluia.

HYMN

O blessèd Lord, Creator God,
In you all things are rendered pure,
By you are strengthened to endure.

O blessèd holy hand of God,
All things are sanctified by you;
Adorned, enriched, you make them new.

O blessèd Majesty of God,
Containing all that you have filled;
All things are done as you have willed.

O blessèd, holy Trinity,
Serene and certain in your ways;
You are the light of endless days.

CONCLUSION

When no other Hour follows and at least in communal recitation:

Let us praise the Lord.
℟ Thanks be to God.